INSIGHT GUIDES

EXPLORE
SICILY

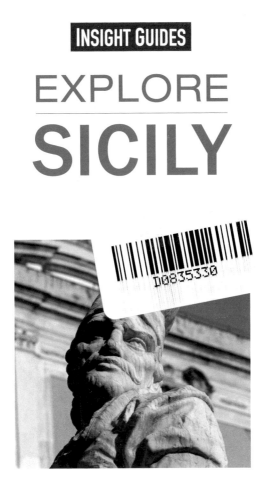

D0835330

CONTENTS

BAROQUE AT ITS BEST

Succumb to Sicilian Baroque in Noto, Ragusa and other cities of the Val di Noto Unesco World Heritage site (Route 10), and see splendid restored Baroque churches and palaces in the centre of Catania (Route 11).

RECOMMENDED ROUTES FOR...

CASTLES

Sweep away the cobwebs by visiting great medieval castles, including those in Erice (Route 5), Enna (Route 8), Siracusa (Route 9) and Catania (Route 11), built by the Normans or Swabians.

ISLAND HOPPERS

Sail on ferries or hydrofoils to the stunningly beautiful Aeolian Islands (Route 14) off the northeast coast, popular for volcano-climbing and viewing, wallowing in mud baths, hiking, sailing and swimming.

MARKETS

The teeming markets of Palermo (Routes 1 and 2) and Catania (Route 11), with mountains of glistening fresh produce and raucous street life, are riveting spectacles. Dive in early to see them at their best.

MOSAIC ART

Admire the Byzantine Norman mosaics in Palermo's Cappella Palatina (Route 1), the cathedrals of Cefalù (Route 3) and Monreale (Route 4), then visit Villa Romana del Casale (Route 8) for superb Roman floor mosaics.

TOP MUSEUMS

Discover outstanding collections of prehistoric and classical archaeological remains in the museums of Agrigento (Route 7), Siracusa (Route 9), Palermo (Route 1) and Lípari (Route 14).

TOP TEMPLES

Sicily has more ancient Greek temples than Greece. Track down the most splendid at Agrigento (Route 7), Segesta (Route 4) and Selinunte (Route 6), and in summer stay for Greek drama under the stars.

VOLCANOES AND VIEWS

Explore Sicily's dramatically active volcanoes: a cable car, trail-bashing jeep tour or climb up Etna (Route 13), a hike up smouldering Vulcano or a view of the exploding cone of Strómboli from the sea (Route 14).

INTRODUCTION

An introduction to Sicily's geography, customs and culture, plus
illuminating background information on cuisine, history and what to do
when you're there.

Sicilian smile

EXPLORE SICILY

Goethe found Sicily intoxicating, from the Classical temples and Etna's eruptions to the volcanic Sicilians themselves. 'To have seen Italy without seeing Sicily', he wrote, 'is not to have seen Italy at all – for Sicily is the key to everything.'

Sicily's strategic maritime setting, at the crossroads of Mediterranean trade routes, has always played a crucial role in the island's history. Phoenicians, Greeks, Carthaginians, Romans, Arabs, Normans and Spaniards all left their mark, embellishing the island with some of their finest works and creating a beguiling cultural hybrid.

The varied legacies are redolent in the complex traditions and customs, as well as the diversity of architectural styles. It's perhaps not surprising that Sicilians see themselves as a separate nation from mainland Italy or the rest of Europe. When they cross the 4km (2.5-mile) Strait of Messina to the Italian peninsula, they're off to '*il Continente*'.

Likewise, mainland Italians see Sicilians as foreigners and northern Italians refer to them as Africans. Many islanders still speak the Sicilian dialect, a rich Romance language sprinkled with words from Latin, Greek, Arabic, French and Spanish. The food – one of the great pleasures of a visit to Sicily – is different too, drawing from the culinary culture of Arabs and other invaders.

Sicily's fascination lies in the unexpected. Mount Etna's smoking plumes hover above scented citrus groves, Greek temple columns support a Baroque cathedral, exotic Arab-Norman churches glow with Byzantine mosaics, city street markets are tinged with the flavour of a Morrocan souk. Sicilian experiences know no bounds. You can ski in the morning, sunbathe in the afternoon, gaze into a bubbling volcanic crater one day, bathe from volcanic rocks the next. Another day you could marvel at mosaics in a Roman emperor's hunting villa, visit a valley of Greek temples or watch a Greek drama unfold in an ancient theatre under the stars.

GEOGRAPHY AND LAYOUT

Lying halfway between Gibraltar and the Suez Canal, Sicily is the largest island in the Mediterranean and Italy's largest region. At 25,708 sq km (9,926 square miles) it is far bigger than most first-time visitors imagine, and while motorways help cut journey times, much of the island is mountainous and slow going. For example,

Tango dancers in Palermo   *Fish market in Catania*

crossing the island from Trápani in the west to Siracusa in the east takes at least four hours, and over five if you avoid the motorway. The landscape, whose diversity is unmatched by other Mediterranean islands, is one of mountains, citrus groves, pastureland and vast expanses of rolling wheat-fields. The scenery is monumentally dramatic around Mount Etna, which dominates, and periodically threatens, the eastern coast. But Sicily is not all scenic. Around many of the cities there are great swathes of unsightly development, much of it modern unregulated blocks built by the Mafia. While some historic sites stand in blissful isolation, others, such as the glorious Greek relics in Agrigento's Valley of the Temples, are encroached upon by the modern world.

To cover the main cities and sights in one trip you'll need a good fortnight and at least two bases. If touring, you'd ideally fly into Palermo or Trápani in the west and out of Catania in the east. The itineraries in the book begin with Palermo (and Cefalù in Palermo province), then move around the coastline in a westerly direction.

The west coast is followed by a tour of the famous temples of Agrigento and an inland foray to hilltop Enna and the Roman Villa at Piazza Armerina. On the east coast, walks are devoted to each of Siracusa, Catania and the popular resort of Taormina, with inland tours of the Baroque gems of the southeast and the foothills of dominant Mount Etna. Last come the glorious Aeolian Islands, which float off the Tyrrhenian coast. All around the island you will see the Trinacria, the ancient symbol of Sicily, which became the official public flag in 2000. It features the head of Medusa with three wheat ears (symbolising the fertile land) and three bent legs (representing the island's three points).

CLIMATE AND WHEN TO VISIT

Sicily enjoys a mild Mediterranean climate, with hot, dry summers. The only extremes you can expect are in July and August, when daytime temperatures average 28°C (82°F). During this period it can be unbearably hot and crowded, especially in August when Italians take their summer holidays. Those choosing to visit in the height of summer should be prepared to spend the hottest hours indoors, or immersed in water. It is always a good idea to take along a pair of sturdy, closed shoes if you are planning to go for a hike on Mount Etna. Generally the best times to go are April, when spring flowers carpet the hillsides, through to early June, then from late September to October/November. During these periods it's cooler and less crowded, and the sea is often still warm in November. Winters along the coast are short and generally

The Sicilian flag with the Trinacria

mild, though a large number of resort hotels and restaurants are closed. In the interior, especially the mountainous areas, temperatures are lower and Mount Etna remains snowcapped until late April or May, often offering marvellous eruptions with lava melting the snow. The Aeolian Islands are subject to strong winds and the main season is relatively short – from June to September.

THE SICILIANS

Islanders see themselves as Sicilian first and Italian second. In his masterpiece *The Leopard*, Giuseppe Tomasi di Lampedusa described them as follows: 'Sicilians never wish to improve for the simple reason that they believe themselves perfect. Their vanity is stronger than their misery. Every invasion by outsiders upsets their illusion of achieved perfection, and risks disturbing their self-satisfied waiting for nothing at all'. Although they have a reputation for being brooding, suspicious and inscrutable, closer contact reveals stoicism, conservatism and deep sensibility. This contradictory character doesn't match the sunny Mediterranean stereotype of *dolce far niente*, but visitors may nonetheless encounter overwhelming hospitality. Whether you're staying in the simplest *agriturismo* (farm-stay), a sumptuous palace with a Baroque ballroom or a boutique wine resort, the generous

Sicilian spirit remains the same. The slightest friendly gesture from a foreigner is rewarded with fresh pastries, a bunch of just-picked grapes, the keys to a long-closed church or an insistence on a tour of an obscure archaeological site. Possibly all at once. Likewise, if you are invited for dinner at a Sicilian home, you are expected to bring wine, pastries or flowers. Food, and the pleasure of eating together, are considered one of the most important aspects of life, so if invited, expect to sit at the table for a long time, and to eat various courses. Common topics of conversation include football and, again, the food itself. In the evening, Sicilians like to meet in the city's piazzas, eating ice cream on a bench or having a drink in front of one of the popular bars.

Appearances matter here, and Sicilian homes will typically be perfectly clean and neat, especially when receiving guests. Sicilian dialect has many words to express this: *azzizzare* (to beautify) comes from Arabic; *orfanità* is Spanish-Palermitan dialect for looking good; *spagnolismo* (Hispanicism) naturally means seeming better than you are. Sicilian society is still predominantly male-based and, in the smaller internal towns, you probably won't see a woman sitting at a bar, as that is considered inappropriate. Women travelling alone can attract appreciative comments or whistles, but these are usually harmless. Critics

Taormina's Teatro Greco   *Castellamare and coastline*

DON'T LEAVE SICILY WITHOUT...

Discovering Sicilian Baroque. Take in the beauty of Sicily's Baroque gems. The area comprising Noto, Scicli, Modica and Ragusa is a Unesco World Heritage site, with churches and palaces created in a wildly theatrical style, characterised by fantasy and ornamentation.

Riding round a smouldering volcano. Take the Circumetnea Railway for a thrilling ride around the base of Mount Etna, or take a trail-bashing jeep tour up the volcano. Offshore, you can hike up Vulcano as it smoulders, or view the exploding cone of Strómboli from the sea.

Visiting some of the finest Greek temples in the world. Sicily has more ancient Greek temples than Greece. The most magnificent are at Agrigento, Segesta and Selinunte; on summer nights, they stage open-air Greek drama performances.

Tasting Sicily's sweet delights. Stemming from their Moorish past, Sicilians have a passion for sweet desserts and confectionery. There are *pasticcerie* galore displaying tempting cakes and pastries, including the mouthwatering ricotta-filled *cannoli* and *cassata siciliana*. The local favourite, *frutti alla Martorana*, are brightly coloured, calorie-loaded peaches, apricots, strawberries and cherries made of pure marzipan. They take their name from the church of La Martorana, where the Benedictine nuns first created them.

Taking a stroll in the chaotic capital Palermo. Both a glorious assault on the senses and the glittering summation of Arab-Norman artistic achievement, Sicily's capital packs a powerful punch with exotic architecture and vibrant street life.

Exploring the island's wild landscape. The Zíngaro Nature Reserve is a stretch of gorgeous unspoilt coastline, skirting idyllic bays and rocky headlands. The Madonie Mountains are popular with hikers, offering fabulous views and lofty medieval villages to discover.

Tasting the street food in Palermo and Catania. The food alone makes a trip to Sicily worthwhile. The island's Arab heritage, volcanic soil and teeming seas have helped create a rich and varied cuisine.

Falling in love with its glittering mosaics. Sicily is mosaic heaven. The Byzantine-Norman mosaics in Palermo's Palatine Chapel and in the cathedrals of Cefalú and Monreale are breathtaking. The Villa Romana has unrivalled floor mosaics.

Taking in a puppet show. Puppet shows are a Sicilian tradition. Their stories are based on the adventures of the knights in Charlemagne's court, and the puppets are exquisitely painted and dressed.

Visiting a wine resort. Sicily has seen an increasing number of appealing wine estates where you can usually stay, dine or do a cookery or wine-tasting course. Just outside Alcamo, the Sirignano Wine Resort is a delightful organic estate run by the Marchese de Gregori. Guests stay in converted farmworkers' cottages and sample the superb wines over meals cooked by an outstanding chef.

Ornate balcony, Noto

claim that Sicilians remain sluggish citizens, subsidy junkies with little sense of self-help. Sicilians reply that power and prestige lie elsewhere. History has taught them to mistrust institutions.

THE MAFIA

The modern Mafia took root in Sicily in the 1860s, ostensibly to help the rural poor have their share of the land reform and other benefits from Unification. In effect, the Mafia became an integral part of the island's power structure, controlling business and the workings of government. By the 1970s, Sicily had emerged as a strategic centre for drugs, arms and international crime. In the early 1980s, a Mafia war left Palermo's streets strewn with blood and the Corleone-based clan undisputed victors.

In response to charges of government complicity a crackdown on the Mafia was launched. Thousands of suspects were rounded up and an anti-Mafia pool of magistrates was assembled. One 'maxi-trial' resulted in no less than 18 life sentences. Two Mafia-fighting magistrates, Giovanni Falcone and Paolo Borsellino, were murdered by the Mafia in 1992. The terror continued in 1993 with bombs in Milan and Rome, as well as an explosion at Florence's Uffizi Gallery.

The atrocities weakened the Mafia's grip on public opinion, its greatest weapon, and dented the age-old code of loyalty.

The new Sicily
In response to changing circumstances the Mafia has gone to ground, abandoning high-profile terror for activities such as money-laundering, arms-dealing, drug-trafficking, protection rackets, embezzlement of EU funds and property speculation. Where once Mafioso activity was seen as revolt against the state, justified by centuries of foreign oppression, today Sicilians are much less tolerant of organised crime, particularly the young generation.

The confiscation of Mafia property continues apace, and there's a genuine grassroots movement calling for change. The Addiopizzo association fights against the payment of *pizzo* (protection money). Since it was founded in 2004, hundreds of businesses across Sicily have signed up. Civic-minded Sicilians also support Libera Terra shops and cooperatives, which sell pasta, oil, cheese and wine produced on confiscated Mafia land.

Sicilians are tired of being associated with the Mafia, and they are now ready to work on Sicily's revamped image. Recent years have seen the resurgence of Palermo, the restoration of Baroque towns – particularly the Unesco-listed gems of southeast Sicily – and the creation of nature reserves to protect areas of outstanding beauty. Chic boutique hotels, seductive farm-

Passeggiata in Erice　　　*Capella Palatina mosaics, Palermo*

stays and wine estates are also part of the exciting new Sicilian landscape.

In the past few years, Sicily has had to face the impact of extensive illegal immigration. Despite high tolls and a high death risk, thousands of migrants every summer leave the coasts of North Africa on old and unsafe ships toward Lampedusa, where they are welcomed by compassionate associations but faced with Italy's immigration laws.

TOP TIPS FOR EXPLORING SICILY

Hiking up Etna. Independent hikers can choose one of the two main routes up Etna: the northern route via Linguaglossa, considered cooler and prettier in terms of scenery, with forests and wild flowers. The southern route, via Nicolosi, is more dramatic with the barren flanks of the volcano scarred by lava flows and gritty fields of clinker. Jeep and trekking trips include hikes around summit craters, the black and desolate Valle del Bove, scene of the main eruptions, the underground lava cave of Grotta del Gelo (Dec–May) and the 2002 eruption zone. Winter hiking in high areas is not possible due to snow and bad visibility.

Sicilian markets. A foray into the raucous and exotic street markets, especially in Palermo and Catania, is a great experience. You'll find everything from slabs of swordfish and live eels to hunks of parmesan, salted capers and sun-dried tomatoes to cheap clothes and crafts. Every Sicilian town of any size holds a market at least once a week.

The Baroque train. The delightful Treno del Barocco is a quaint vintage train running from Siracusa to Ragusa and back, stopping off in Noto, Scicli, Módica and Ragusa Ibla. Trains run on Sundays only from late spring to October. For information visit www. treno-barocco.blogspot.co.uk or email: uffi-cio.turistico@comune.modica.rg.it.

Chocolate box. Módica is famous for its chocolate, which is very sweet, slightly gritty and comes in all sorts of flavours. You can sample it, along with an irresistible range of cakes and pastries, at Bonajuto at Corso Umberto I No. 159, down a side street almost opposite the church of San Pietro. As well as chocolate bars there are *impanatigghi*, pastries made with chocolate and meat (not that you'd know), *testa di Moro*, fried pastry filled with chocolate custard, and *cannoli* pastries, filled with sweet ricotta cheese and chocolate.

Catania by bus. If pushed for time in Catania, consider the hop-on-hop-off, multi-language bus tour (www.katanelive.it) which costs €6.

Summer festivals in Taormina. The tourist office in Palazzo Corvaja provides information on all the seasonal cultural events happening at the Greek Theatre. The Taormina Film Festival (www.taorminafilmfest.it) in June is one of the highlights of the year, drawing big international names.

Fresh anchovies, Catania market

FOOD AND DRINK

The food alone makes a trip to Sicily worthwhile. The island's Arab heritage, fertile volcanic soil and teeming seas have supplied the islanders with a rich and varied cuisine. This is complemented by an impressive selection of wines.

One of Sicily's best-kept secrets is its cuisine. Only a few local dishes, such as the sweet-and-sour aubergine side dish known as *caponata* or ricotta-filled *cannoli*, have crossed the Strait of Messina to find fame and fortune abroad.

The Greek colonists who arrived in the 8th century BC were astonished at the fertility of Sicily's volcanic soil, and Siracusa soon became the gastronomic capital of the Classical world. By the 5th century BC the city had given birth to the first cookbook written in the West, Mithaecus' *Lost Art of Cooking*, and also to the first school for chefs.

The Arabs set the mould of Sicilian cooking, introducing aubergines, citrus fruits and rice, along with a sweet and spicy cuisine. Cane sugar was introduced, as was the Middle Eastern taste for sumptuous sweets – still a classic Sicilian trademark.

Until the Renaissance, the island exported pasta, sugar, confectionery and citrus to northern Italy. But while the Spanish brought chocolate and tomatoes from the New World and French chefs refined the raw ingredients, Sicilian cuisine reflected class lines. The poor survived on bread, beans and broth, the

nobility dined on lavish 'baronial cuisine' from plates of gold and silver. The cooking typical of Sicily today is a combination of the traditions of the rich and poor, but always dedicated to exalting the extraordinary flavours of the produce.

LOCAL CUISINE

Palermo relishes a blood-and-guts cuisine, with such staples as *milza* (spleen) and chicken giblets. In western Sicily, Arab influences prevail, both in Trápani's *cuscus* and in dishes made with pine nuts and raisins. Agrigento prides itself on its *coniglio all'agrodolce* – sweet-and-sour rabbit with aubergines, capers, olives and wine. Around Etna, specialities include pasta with wild mushrooms and herby sausages, while in the hilly interior salami and cow's cheeses are common.

WHERE TO EAT AND DRINK

Traditionally a *ristorante* is smarter and more expensive than a *trattoria* or *osteria*, but these days there is little difference between them. Pizzerias are plentiful. The best use wood-fired ovens

Sicilian wine

Olives are a staple

(forno a legna), but these are sometimes open only in the evening. A *tavola calda* or *rosticceria* are both café-style eateries where hot dishes are prepared daily.

Cafés and bars are a way of life for Italians, from the breakfast *cappuccino* and *cornetto* to the lunchtime snack and coffee to the evening *aperitivo*. In summer, Sicilians will start their day by dipping a soft Sicilian *brioche* in their coffee-flavoured *granita* (crushed ice). Along with wines and often a great range of cocktails and liqueurs, bars also serve pastries, bread rolls, sandwiches and other snacks. An *enoteca* (wine bar) will offer a platter of sliced *prosciutto crudo*, salami or cheese to accompany its wide choice of fine wines.

WHAT TO EAT

Antipasti (starters)

For starters Sicily offers an array of vegetables, from peppers in oil *(peperonata)* to stuffed tomatoes *(pomodori ripieni)*. Aubergines are a staple, whether grilled, fried, rolled and stuffed *(involtini di melanzane)* or baked in a parmesan and tomato sauce *(melanzane alla parmigiana)*.

A classic dish is *caponata*, featuring fried peppers, aubergines, tomatoes, courgettes, celery and olives. The sea provides inspiration for the classic *insalata di mare*, a seafood salad tossed in a dressing of oil, lemon and herbs, and *pesce spada affumicato* (smoked swordfish).

Il primo (first course)

Under the Arabs, Sicily was the first place to produce dried pasta on a commercial scale. The best-loved dish is *pasta alla Norma* (after the heroine in the opera by native son Bellini). Here tomatoes, basil, fried aubergines and a sprinkling of salted ricotta melt into a magical blend. Equally famous is *pasta con le sarde*, invented in the 9th century by Arab army cooks who used whatever was at hand: sardines, saffron, pine nuts, dried currants and sprigs of wild fennel.

Pasta is served with a wide variety of seafood sauces, from clams *(alle vongole)* and sea urchins *(ai ricci)* to prawns *(ai gamberi)* and cuttlefish ink *(al nero di seppia)*. Pasta can also be paired with *fritella*, a spring sauté of new peas, fava beans and tiny artichokes, or simpler combinations garnished with sautéed courgettes. In the Trápani area, where the Arab influence is strongest, a local version of couscous, steamed in a fish broth, supplants pasta. This is best tasted during the vibrant September Couscous Festival at San Vito lo Capo.

Il secondo (main course)

Fish and seafood predominate in Sicily and, apart from in the interior, are generally a better bet than meat. On the coast, fresh grilled fish, mussels and *risotto marinara* (seafood risotto) are rarely bettered. *Sarde a beccafico* – filleted sardines stuffed with cheese, garlic, parsley and capers – are on

most menus. For simpler tastes try a grilled swordfish steak *(pesce spada)* or tuna *(tonno)*. The mountain pastures of Madonie and Nebrodi produce exceptional lamb and pork. Beef is best stuffed and braised in tomato sauce or skewered and grilled *(involtini alla siciliana)*. In the interior, *impanata* is a popular pie with goat or lamb in a parsley and garlic sauce. *Incasciata* is made with sausage, broccoli, raisins, garlic and pine nuts.

Contorni (vegetables)

Vegetables in antipasti are nearly always delicious, but cooked vegetables and mixed salad are often a disappointment, especially when you see the wonderful locally grown produce in markets. *Peperonata* and *melanzane alla parmigiana* (see under *Antipasti*) reign supreme. Orange and fennel salad is a legacy of the Arabs; artichokes come fried, stuffed, roasted on coals, or braised with oil, parsley and garlic. The interior boasts a survivor from Classical times, *maccu*, which is a purée made from dried fava or broad beans flavoured with oil and wild fennel seeds.

Street food

Sicily has a long tradition of cheap snacks eaten on the hoof, especially in Palermo and Catania. Chickpea fritters and bread *(pane e panelle)*, potato croquettes, with anchovy and *caciocavallo* cheese *(crocchette di patate)*, grilled goat's intestine filled with onions, cheese, egg and parsley *(stigghiola)*, fried rice balls filled with chopped meat and peas *(arancini)*, and beef spleen or tripe roll *(pani cu'la meusa)* provide a movable feast of typically local taste. Look for food trucks in Palermo and Catania.

Food markets are the best sources of street food, especially in Palermo and Catania. Street snacks can also be seriously sweet: *frutta alla Martorana* (decorated marzipan fruits), Enna's speciality of *le sfingi* (rice-flour doughnuts drenched in honey) or the ubiquitous *cannoli* (see under *Dolci*).

Dolci (desserts)

The Arab inheritance is reflected in spicy fruit jellies, sorbets and *cassata siciliana*, a cloyingly sweet sponge cake with almond paste and candied peel. In general, Sicilian patisserie is elaborate in appearance and sophisticated in flavour, combining the taste of citrus fruits with sweet cheeses, dried fruit and almonds.

Cannoli are crisp, sweet, tube-shaped pastries stuffed with ricotta and candied fruit. It's the classic island favourite and can be found in every *pasticceria* along with *pasta reale* (marzipan fruits) and *pasta di mandorle* (almond cakes). Fruit, ricotta, honey, almonds and pistachio nuts often flavour cakes and ice cream. Ice cream is a reason for pride among Sicilians: made with fresh fruits and usually no preservatives, the low-fat Sicilian gelato is said to have been

Sicilian pastries are a speciality

invented by the Arabs who mixed snow from the peaks of the Etna with fresh fruit and sugar, and is more delicate in flavour than Italian gelato. A traditional August dessert is *gelo di melone*, a watermelon jelly pudding with chocolate seeds.

DRINKS

Vino (wine)

Sicilian wines have a great pedigree, dating back to Phoenician and Greek times, but have traditionally underperformed. With their prodigious sugar content, they were dispatched north for blending to bump up the strength of better-known wines. More recently, though, there has been a full-scale return to producing serious drinking wines, and to harnessing native grape varieties to that end.

Good-quality reds are made from the local Nero d'Avola grape variety; look out too for the dry red Cerasuolo di Vittoria from Ragusa province, the dry whites from Alcamo in the west and the up-and-coming new wines from the lava-enriched foothills of Etna. *Trattorie* will often sell house wines in jugs, available by the *litro* (litre), *mezzo* litro (half-litre) and *quarto di litro* (quarter-litre). The wine varies hugely but can be surprisingly decent, and will cost a good deal less than branded wines. Ask for the *vino della casa*.

Sicily's best-known wine is Marsala. It's still mistakenly synonymous with cheap, sickly-sweet liqueurs (see page 55), but the best (known as *Vergine* or *Riserva*) are excellent dry, smooth, sherry-like wines. Sweet elixirs, in fact, are something of a Sicilian speciality. The island of Pantelleria produces Moscato di Pantelleria Naturale, made from Zibibbo grapes, while the island of Salina has a similar tradition but with Malvasia rather than Moscato vines, and Taormina produces Vino alla Mandorla, a wine made from crushed almonds.

Soft drinks

For a sure-fire remedy for the effects of summer heat try a *spremuta*, a freshly squeezed juice made with oranges *(arance)* or lemons *(limoni)*. Another refreshing Sicilian speciality is *granita*, a drink of crushed ice flavoured with the fresh juice of lemons, strawberries, other seasonal fruits or sometimes even sweetened coffee. Try mulberry *(mora)*, peach *(pesca)* or watermelon *(anguria)*. Sicilians also like to drink *Chinotto*, a dark-coloured carbonated soft drink produced from the fruit of the myrtle-leaved orange tree, which is only cultivated in the Taormina area. An especially popular drink in the Catania area is *seltz*, a mix of sweet fruit syrup and tonic water. Order a glass of the colourful drink from a *ciospo*, one of the old kiosks you'll find on street corners around town. Tangerine and lemon *(mandarino al limone)* is the most famous flavour.

Kitsch souvenirs

SHOPPING

Sicily may not be as chic as mainland Italy, but that's part of its charm. Pottery, puppets, papyrus and coral jewellery represent the best of traditional Sicilian handicrafts, while volcanic rock and sulphur crystals make excellent souvenirs.

Although Sicily now has its first luxury designer mall (see Fashion), shopping on the island is less about Gucci or Armani and more about atmospheric street markets, ceramic workshops, black lava souvenirs and gastronomy.

There are food temptations wherever you go: chocolate from Módica, pastries from Noto, pistachios from Bronte and capers from the Aeolian Islands.

SHOPPING HOURS

Opening times are Mon–Sat 8/9am–1pm and 4–7.30pm, but many non-food shops close on Mondays and, with the exception of supermarkets, food shops usually close on Wednesdays. In Taormina, the shops are open daily.

ANTIQUES

Siracusa is renowned for its reproductions of Classical Greek coins. Palermo offers treasures, fakes and junk at its daily antiques market near the Cappuccini Catacombs, while the shops around Corso Umberto sell a mixture of antiques and bric-a-brac. In antiques markets what you see is rarely genuine.

Some of the most distinctive items in antiques shops are parts of the painted carts *(carretti siciliani)* that were once the mainstay of transport in the countryside. Intact carts are now collectors' items.

POTTERY AND CERAMICS

Sicilian terracotta pottery dates back to Classical times, but the sophisticated Persian glazing techniques were introduced by the Arabs in the 9th century.

Today the best ceramic workshops are found in Santo Stefano di Camastra and in Caltagirone. Santo Stefano sells a range of ceramics, but the authentic ware has a rustic look, often with fish motifs. Caltagirone ceramics have distinct animal and floral motifs in dark blue and copper green with splashes of yellow. Look out for the tall *albarelli* jars once used for storing dry drugs, and the vast array of heads depicting characters from Sicilian history that are used as ornaments or flower pots.

PAPYRUS

The ancient Egyptians brought the African plant of papyrus to Siracusa, and

Antiques and bric-a-brac   *Pottery maker in Santo Stefano*

Fonte Ciane near the city is now the only place in Europe where it grows wild. The Museo del Papiro in Siracusa (see page 70) has samples of ancient papyrus art. Stalls and shops all over the town sell inexpensive papyrus pictures, from fine copies of Egyptian designs to tacky portraits while you wait.

CRAFTS

Erice produces bright, hand-woven cotton rugs. Monreale is known for straw and cane goods. Palermo, Catania and Taormina are home to jewellers selling coral and gold.

Or you can buy replicas of the puppets from Sicily's popular puppet theatres – puppetry's main traditions are in Palermo and some of the best models are still made there. **Vincenzo Argento**, the last puppet maker in a 160-year-old family business, will make a *paladino* (paladin or knight) to order (Corso Vittorio Emanuele 445, Palermo; tel: 091 611 3680).

FOOD AND WINE

Look out for delis selling local specialities such as fruit preserves, almond spreads, spicy pesto, salted tuna roe *(bottarga)*, honey, olive oil and salted capers. Sicilian pastries such as *cannoli* (see page 16) and almond cakes are abundant. Seasonal sweets and biscuits include marzipan lambs for Easter and *ossi dei morti* (dead men's bones) biscuits for All Souls. In Palermo, *pupa a cera* are fig-

ures made of icing sugar. A green tangerine fruit syrup from a Catanese *ciospo* (kiosk), or a pistachio pesto from a speciality shop, make for perfect gifts.

Local wines can be tasted in an *enoteca* (wine shop), which acts as a regional showcase. In Taormina you'll find the local *vino alla mandorla* (sweet wine flavoured with almonds) as well as dessert wine, especially Moscato and Malvasia from the volcanic islands.

FASHION

Sicilia Outlet Village (www.siciliaoutlet village.it) in Agira, just east of Enna, is Sicily's first luxury designer shopping mall. Fashions here are heavily discounted. Free shuttles run from Palermo, Messina and Trápani. For fashion elsewhere head to the boutiques of Taormina, Palermo (Viale della Libertà and Via Ruggero Settimo) or Catania (Via Etnea). Here you'll find designer clothes from Valentino, Coveri, Gucci, Armani and the half-Sicilian Dolce & Gabbana. For cheaper clothes in Palermo try Via Maqueda or Via Roma, and in Catania opt for the side streets.

ANTI-MAFIA SHOPPING

Libera Terra (www.liberaterra.it), which farms land confiscated from the Mafia, sells produce such as wine, oil and preserves at its shops in Palermo (Piazza Castelnuovo 13), Erice (Via San Rocco 1) and Corleone (Cortile Colletti 2).

Teatro Massimo, Palermo's opera house

ENTERTAINMENT

Catch a concert or puppet show in Palermo, an alfresco classical drama in a Greek theatre, or listen to live music in Catania's late-night bars. For a quiet evening just enjoy the passeggiata (evening stroll) and a glass of Marsala in a local bar.

Palermo and Catania offer a great season of opera, ballet and concerts (see page 120). Catania suits a young crowd, with its late-night bars and live music venues. Palermo empties on summer evenings, when the locals decamp to the beach resort of Mondello for the nightly fashion parade and fine dining. For the most sophisticated nightlife, head to glitzy Taormina and join the chic set over cocktails at the grand hotels. If your visit coincides with one of the many festivals, be sure to leap in and cast inhibitions aside.

CLASSICAL DRAMA

Sicily's classical theatres often return to their original function as great settings for ancient Greek drama. Between May and June different dramatic cycles are performed in the Greek amphitheatres, from Siracusa and Segesta to Selinunte, Agrigento and Morgantina. In Taormina, the Greco-Roman theatre (see page 81) is the spectacular setting for an annual summer arts festival in July and August which includes classical drama as well as opera, dance and music.

FILM

Sicily has a fascinating cinematic heritage. Major movies featuring Sicily include *The Godfather* trilogy, *Cinema Paradiso* (1988), *The Leopard* (1963), based on Giuseppe di Lampedusa's eponymous bestseller, *Il Postino* (1994), *Stròmboli: Terra di Dio* (1949) and more recently the Montalbano films and TV series, based on novels by Italy's best-selling author, Andrea Camilleri.

In the Footsteps of The Godfather is one of the most popular trails from Taormina and can be done independently with a visit to the villages of Forza d'Agro and Savoca, where *The Godfather* was filmed. In Palermo you can book a tour of the Teatro Massimo, where the melodramatic massacre in *The Godfather III* was filmed. The Montalbano Trail in the southeast takes you to towns and seaside spots which feature in the detective series.

FESTIVALS

Sicily has festivals for every season. A matter of great local pride, these are a mix of pagan and Christian, magic and

Puppet show in Siracusa   *Tribute to Francis Ford Coppola, Savocca*

music, folklore and feasting. *Carnevale* marks the beginning of Lent and a period of abstinence but is celebrated in many places with licentious abandon.

Easter sees the most activity and is celebrated with processions of holy relics, re-enactments of the Passion or respects paid to Our Lady of the Sorrows. In Enna on Good Friday, 2,000 hooded penitents from medieval fraternities hold a silent procession; in Trápani the Easter procession tours the town for 20 hours non-stop. Palermo's glittering festival of U Fistinu in July celebrates the patron saint, Santa Rosalia, with six days of processions, fireworks and general mayhem.

Among the secular celebrations are Piazza Armerina's Palio dei Normanni, a medieval pageant (mid-August), Agrigento's Sagra del Mandorlo in Fiore, celebrating the almond blossom (February), and Módica's Chocobarocco (late autumn) – a chocolate extravaganza.

NIGHTLIFE

Catania celebrates a vibrant arts scene, offering a rich summer program of classical, live jazz and blues concerts. The nightlife is the best in Sicily, with a profusion of trendy galleries, bars, restaurants and clubs. As an energetic university city, Catania offers events ranging from pop-rock spectaculars to open-air summer festivals. The venues vary from converted refineries to cosy clubs in the city centre. Palermo's nightlife is less developed and some of the areas where the bars and restaurants are located are not particularly safe at night. The safest and liveliest piazzas are Piazza Castelnuovo and Piazza Verdi. In all of the smaller towns, it is traditional to spend the evening in the main piazza, usually in front of one of the bars, whereas clubs are often slightly out of town.

Puppet theatre

Travelling puppet shows have been a form of entertainment in Sicily for centuries. The tales are in Italian and are usually based on the exploits of knights in Charlemagne's court, but even if you don't understand Italian there's plenty to enjoy. Puppets are exquisitely painted and dressed and some, at 1.5m (5ft) tall, are almost life-size. Mimmo Cuticchio, from an old puppeteering family, is one of the few remaining highly skilled raconteurs of Sicilian stories. In Palermo the Museo Internazionale delle Marionette (see page 38) regularly stages performances, and puppet plays can also be seen in Acireale, Catania and Siracusa. Palermo's Teatro di Via Bara (www.figlidarte-cuticchio.com) presents reinterpreted versions of traditional puppet theatre. Travelling puppet shows tour the island in summer; ask at local tourist offices for details.

Trekking in the Alacantara gorge, near Etna

OUTDOOR ACTIVITIES

Sicily holds increasing appeal for active visitors. The diversity of landscape, from mountains and volcanoes to tiny islands and beaches, is unmatched by other Mediterranean islands and provides myriad opportunities for active pursuits.

Coasts, islands and mountains lend themselves to year-round sporting activities. You can hike in the hills and mountains, explore the undersea world, quad bike on Etna, wade through gorges and explore offshore islands. For the adventurous there are hikes up active volcanoes – with nightly fireworks in the case of Strómboli. Along with skiing and hiking, Etna now offers gorge-trekking, mountain-biking, motorbiking and bone-shaking jeep ascents.

BEACHES

Unlike Sardinia, Sicily is by no means overrun by swathes of soft sand – some of the best bathing is from coves or rocks, with deep water for diving. The offshore islands have lovely, often volcanic beaches, notably on Ustica, the Egadi and Aeolian Islands. Beaches south of Siracusa are wild and unspoilt, while those between Catania and Taormina tend to be rocky and exciting – though not ideal for swimming or young children. The sea is delightful from May to October, but out of season (November to March) rough waters may bring debris ashore. In high season the easily accessible beaches in the main resorts, particularly on the north coast, are invariably packed.

WATER SPORTS

Rich in flora and fauna, the coasts are excellent for diving and snorkelling, especially off the rocky shorelines on the smaller islands and along the northern coast.

Ustica, home to a natural marine reserve, has spectacular diving in deep water around the remains of a wreck. Isola Bella, a tiny island off Taormina, as well as Marettimo on the Egadi Islands, are favourites with snorkellers and divers. The Aeolian Islands are perfect for sailing, but mainland Sicily is not well equipped for sailors. The best spots for windsurfing are on the south coast where a strong, dry wind often blows.

HIKING

Sicily's rugged terrain is well suited to hiking, though there are relatively few established trails. Increasingly popular regions are the Nebrodi and Madonie mountains, both of which offer challenging hikes. In the Madonie trails

Hiking up on Vulcano

ascend to the peak of Pizzo Carbonara (1,979m/6,495ft), and the mountains here have rich limestone flora with many rare species.

The Riserva Naturale dello Zíngaro (see page 46) is the most well-designed reserve, with trails along the coast via tiny coves with crystal waters, and paths cutting through forest-covered mountainsides. The volcanic landscapes of Etna exert an obvious pull for hikers, but it's advisable to take a guide and to wear sturdy shoes. (See page 85 for information on exploring Etna.) The Alcantara gorge also provides fascinating hiking adventures, both in-water and around the gorge itself, whose geometric rocky formations were formed by runoff from Mount Etna. The Aeolian and Egadi islands offer excellent opportunities for hiking, from climbing the craters of Vulcano and Strómboli to off-the-beaten track exploration of remote Filicudi or Maréttimo. Summer heat often becomes unbearable from 11am, so hikers should start early in the morning.

SKIING

Sicily is not renowned for skiing, but its highest peaks have lifts and other facilities. Recent eruptions from Etna, especially in 2012, have caused the skiing areas to close, but the season normally runs from December to March.

Etna's ski resorts are Linguaglossa on the northern side and Nicolosi on the southern side. Both resorts are suitable for intermediate and expert skiers, but Linguaglossa is the better choice for beginners. The views are spectacular, and of course there is an element of bravado in the idea of skiing on a live volcano.

In the Madonie mountains, the main ski resort is the alpine village of Piano Battaglia.

CYCLING

Leisure cycling has yet really to take off on mainland Sicily, but demand has risen from visitors in recent years. Typical bike tours offered by agencies include Etna, the Val di Noto, the Marsala coast or the offshore islands, where cycling is particularly popular (perhaps because it's flatter) and reflects the slower pace of life.

Specialist UK cycle tour operators, such as Headwater (www.headwater.com), offer self-guided and group guided tours. Most of the offshore islands have mountain bikes to rent at the ports.

GOLF

Sicily has a handful of golf resorts, the most luxurious of which is Verdura Golf & Spa Resort, near Sciacca (www.verduraresort.com). The most established club, Il Picciolo (www.ilpicciologolf.com), is an 18-hole, par-72 course on the slopes of Mount Etna. The terrain is pretty challenging, and play can be suspended if lava flows threaten to reach the course.

Greek ruins in Selinunte

CULTURE AND HISTORY

Sicily's great source of fascination is the range and quality of monuments that illustrate its complex history. The classical temples, Moorish palaces, Swabian castles and Baroque palazzi lend a theatrical and unique presence to the island.

Sicily's history is a cavalcade of invasion by ancient tribes. The Sicani, Siculi and Ęlymni were the first settlers; then came the Carthaginians and Greeks, the Romans, Arabs, mercenaries and slaves, Vandals, Goths, Saracens, Normans and Spaniards. Most remained for long periods, adding rich layers to Sicily's extraordinary fusion of genes and culture. Of the three great ancient civilisations that held sway in Sicily, the Greeks left the most enduring architectural legacy. The Carthaginians' buildings and artefacts were largely destroyed by the Greeks, and little remains of Roman temples and public buildings.

EARLY SETTLERS

In the 9th century BC, seafaring Phoenicians colonised northwestern Sicily from the island of Mozia, which retains its Phoenician port and sacrificial burial grounds. The Phoenicians soon came into conflict with Greeks who were tempted to Sicily by its fertile lands, trade and supply of slave labour, settling on the east coast at Naxos in 734 BC. From their colonies in Siracusa and the east coast, the Greeks spread across the island. Siracusa became the cultural capital of the ancient world and the supreme power of Sicily, while the Dorian Greek colonies of Agrigento and Selinunte were two of the richest cities, their temples testifying to their wealth and grandeur.

Romans, Arabs and Normans

The Romans treated Sicily as a Greek treasure trove and an imperial playground. They may not have matched the lovely sites of Magna Graecia, but the Romans built temples and public buildings and left a legacy of sumptuous mosaics. A tantalising glimpse of Sicily as the playground of rich Romans is the Villa Romana at Casale (see page 65), where mosaics illustrate a phantasmagoria of bathing, dancing, fishing, hunting, music and drama.

After the fall of Rome, Siracusa briefly became the capital of Byzantium, and by the 9th century Arabs, Berbers and Spanish Muslims added a patina in the form of Moorish palaces, Arab imagery and freedom of worship. The Arab hallmarks were engineering, irrigation, the introduction of sugar cane and cot-

Mosaics in Monreale   *Sumptuous Baroque in Palermo*

ton, as well as coral- and tuna-fishing. Palermo was by now the most cosmopolitan city in Europe.

Arab liberalism paved the way for the Norman golden age, a period of expansion, enlightenment, prosperity and cultural riches. Count Roger, an itinerant Norman knight, captured Palermo in 1072 and ruled Sicily as an oriental sultan, as did his son Roger II. The cities were graced by Arab-Norman churches and ringed by palms, vineyards, citrus groves and silk farms. Palermo's jewel box, the Cappella Palatina, and the cathedrals in Monreale and Cefalù display the fusion of Arab and Christian, and reflect the Norman inheritance.

A descendent of Roger II, Frederick II von Hohenstaufen (1194–1250), King of Sicily and Holy Roman Emperor, was one of the most brilliant rulers in medieval history. A man of remarkable culture and ability, he introduced a unified legal system, was a patron of science and the arts, and spoke six languages fluently. He wrote poetry and a book on falconry, and studied science, pondering such arcane questions as the workings of Mount Etna and the precise location of hell. Called Stupor Mundi, the Wonder of the World, his legacy to the island is, however, no more than a few forbidding royal fortresses.

Spanish rule
Almost five centuries of Spanish rule followed, when Sicily was isolated from the European mainstream. The aristocracy acquired a taste for *spagnolismo*, the pomp and circumstance associated with Spain.

After a devastating earthquake in 1693, much of eastern and southern Sicily was rebuilt in the Sicilian Baroque style. The eastern Baroque was sober – a mood underscored by the dark lava-stone churches – but that in the south was theatrical and symmetrical, while Palermitan Baroque was sumptuous, in the Spanish style.

From Unification to the present
A period of unrest, when Sicily once again became a pawn of foreign powers, set the stage for Garibaldi's campaign to liberate Sicily from the Bourbons and begin the Unification of the Kingdom of Italy. However, Italian independence brought little benefit to Sicily, merely exchanging the Bourbon viceroys for bureaucrats in Rome.

The Allied occupation of Sicily in 1943, codenamed Operation Husky, was another grim episode, one that unwittingly encouraged the revival of the Mafia by bringing Mafia bosses from New York to raise Sicilian help in defeating the Germans. Huge swathes of unregulated building fattened Mafia coffers.

More recently, an increasing number of Sicilians have been taking an anti-Mafia stand, and lands confiscated from the Mafia are being used for the common good.

Relief of Count Roger

HISTORY: KEY DATES

'Sicily is the schoolroom model for beginners, with every Italian quality and defect magnified, exasperated and highly coloured.' This view by the Italian commentator Luigi Barzini is supported by the bewildering legacy of Sicilian history.

EARLY HISTORY

20,000–10,000 BC	Cave dwellers settle on Sicily.
*c.***1250 BC**	The Siculi (Sicels), Sicani (Sicans) and Elymni (Elymians) settle.
*c.***860 BC**	Carthaginians establish trading posts at Panormus (modern Palermo), Solus (Solunto) and Motya (Mozia).
*c.***733 BC**	Corinthian Greeks found Siracusa.
730–700 BC	Greek colonies created at Megara Hyblaea, Gela, Selinus (modern Selinunte) and Akragas (Agrigento).
5th century BC	Peak of Greek civilisation. Siracusa rivals Athens in power and prestige.
264–241 BC	First Punic War ends in Roman domination of Sicily.
212 BC	Siracusa falls to the Romans.
AD 395	Sicily passes to the Western Roman Empire.
468	Start of barbarian invasions.
535	Byzantines retake Sicily for the Empire.

MEDIEVAL SICILY

831	Palermo falls to the Arabs.
End of 8th century	Sicily under Arab control. Arab colonisation ushers in a golden age for Sicily. The new capital, Palermo, becomes a prosperous centre of scholarship and art, second only to Constantinople.
1061	The Normans land in Sicily: the struggle against the Arabs.
1071	Norman Count Roger takes Palermo 'for Christendom'.
1130	Count Roger's son, Roger II, becomes King of Sicily.
1198–1250	Hohenstaufen Emperor Frederick II expels Arabs and rules Sicily.
1266	Charles of Anjou becomes king and conquers Hohenstaufens.
1282	Sicilian Vespers uprising ousts the French and installs the Spanish.

Depiction of Palermo in 1860 being attacked by Bourbons

SPANISH RULE TO UNIFICATION

1442	Alfonso V of Sicily takes Naples.
1669	Etna erupts, destroying Catania and east coast towns.
1693	Massive earthquake strikes the east.
1713	Treaty of Utrecht. Victor Amadeus II of Piedmont-Savoy becomes King of Sicily.
1734–1860	Spanish Bourbons rule Sicily through viceroys.
1806–15	British occupation of Sicily.
1848–9	Sicilian Revolution.
1860	Garibaldi and his men land at Marsala and defeat the Bourbons.
1861	Sicily joins the newly declared Kingdom of Italy.
1890	Catania inaugurates the Teatro Massimo Vincenzo Bellini

MODERN SICILY

1908	Messina destroyed by an earthquake, with 80,000 victims.
1915	Italy joins the Allies in World War I.
1943	Allied invasion of Sicily.
1946	Sicily is granted regional autonomy.
1951–75	One million Sicilians emigrate, especially to the United States.
1986	The Mafia maxi-trials *(maxiprocessi)* indict hundreds.
1992	The Mafia assassinate two judges Falcone and Borsellino.
1995	Giulio Andreotti, seven times Prime Minister of Italy, faces charges of collaborating with the Mafia.
2006	Mafia boss Bernardo Provenzano is caught after 43 years in hiding.
2010	In Palermo, Pope Benedict XVI preaches against the Mafia.
2011	20,000 Tunisians arrive on the island of Lampedusa. Italian 'technocratic' government replaces Berlusconi.
2012	In November, openly gay anti-mafia centre-left candidate Rosario Crocetta is elected Regional President.
2013	Pope Benedict XVI resigns in February. Before Easter, the Church elects Pope Francis I, who later in the year visits Lampedusa to commemorate thousands of migrants who have died crossing the sea from North Africa. In summer, the new airport of Comiso (near Catania) is inaugurated.
2014	Mount Etna erupts several times in dramatic fashion.

BEST ROUTES

Piazza Pretoria statue

WESTERN PALERMO

Exotic Arab–Norman architecture and a vibrant street market dazzle the senses on this day tour of Palermo. From the Baroque heart of the city the walk takes you through the ancient Albergheria quarter, and on to Palazzo dei Normanni, with its glittering Palatine Chapel.

DISTANCE: 3km (2 miles)
TIME: A full day
START: Quattro Canti
END: Cattedrale
POINTS TO NOTE: Binoculars are useful for the mosaics in the Cappella Palatina. The light in the chapel is constantly changing. Best times to go are late afternoon (as per the itinerary) or mid-morning. Watch your valuables in the market.

Chaotic and gritty, Sicily's capital is a patchwork of periods and styles. In the Middle Ages, when Arab, Norman and Hohenstaufen rulers held sway, it was one of the most prosperous and enlightened cities in the Mediterranean – a melting-pot for Latin, Byzantine and Islamic cultures. Today the historic centre fuses ancient splendour with modern poverty and chaos. With its endless roar of traffic the city does not always endear itself to the first-time visitor, but it is worth persevering to discover some of the finest cultural treasures in Sicily.

After decades of neglect, Palermo is on the up; churches, museums and palaces have recently undergone or are under-going restoration, cultural centres and galleries have opened, and the long–neglected seafront has been rebuilt with a proper promenade and gardens.

Get your bearings at **Quattro Canti** ❶, the heart of the city where the 'four corners' of the old centre are formed by two great arteries, **Via Maqueda** and **Corso Vittorio Emanuele**. The noble crossroads, decorated with symbolic Baroque statuary and fountains, is hard to admire with the roar of the traffic, so head for the more peaceful Piazza Pretoria just off Via Maqueda.

PIAZZA PRETORIA

The Baroque **Piazza Pretoria** ❷ was once disparagingly nicknamed *Piazza della Vergogna* (Square of Shame), after the abundant saucy nudes who frolic in the fountain's spray. This magnificently restored Mannerist pool, designed in the mid-1500s, has over 30 naked or near-naked tritons, nymphs and river

Palermo Cathedral

gods of varying size and quality.

The piazza is overshadowed on one side by the huge domed church of **Santa Caterina**, and on the south side by the **Palazzo delle Aquile**, the town hall named after the stone eagles which decorate its facade.

LA MARTORANA AND SAN CATALDO

Further along Via Maqueda, **Piazza Bellini ❸** is graced with the three little red domes of the chapel of San Cataldo and the 12th-century campanile of **La Martorana ❹** (daily 9am–noon; Wed & Fri 3–6pm). Founded in 1143 by George of Antioch, King Roger's Syrian emir, the church is a remarkable mix of Baroque and Arab-Norman. Although brought up in the Orthodox faith, the emir planned La Martorana as a mosque, yet adorned it with Greek Byzantine mosaics: one depicts the founder, while another shows Christ's Coronation of Roger II. Today, La Martorana is the co-Cathedral of the Catholic Church of Byzantine rite in Sicily, serving an Albanian ethnic minority. The Church of **San Cataldo ❺** (Mon–Sat 12.30am–2pm, 5–8pm; charge), a simple cube topped by red domes and flanked by palms, is one of the last sacred buildings built in the Arab-Norman style.

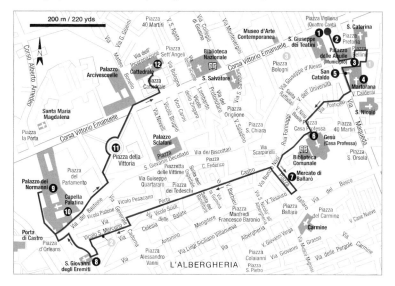

Chiesa del Gesù splendour

Pause for coffee or a cooling drink at **Pizzeria Bellini**, see ➊, on the piazza with a rare view (and top-notch pizzas). Marlon Brando ate here while he was on location for *The Godfather*.

THE ALBERGHERIA QUARTER

Extending south and west of Piazza Bellini are the streets and alleys of the old **Albergheria** quarter, one of the city's poorest districts but once the home of Norman court officials and rich merchants from Pisa and Amalfi. Although many dilapidated houses are home to illegal immigrants, a sense of community prevails over scenes of urban decay. Go south along Via Maqueda from Piazza Bellini, and take Via Ponticello, the first turning on your right. On Piazza Casa Professa the **Chiesa del Gesù** ➏ (daily 9.30am–1.30pm) was founded in the late 16th century as the first Jesuit church in Sicily, its interior a swirl of Baroque excess.

Follow signs for the **Mercato di Ballarò** ➐, Palermo's liveliest daily market. Although less famous than the Vucciria market, Ballaró maintains its ancient character and has a more authentic flavour. It is raucous, sprawling and exotic, with the spicy scents and sounds that transport you back to Moorish times. There are mountains of lemons and oranges, slabs of tuna and swordfish, hanging lamb's heads, pigs' trotters, tripe and intestines, and stallholders screaming everywhere. Side streets are packed with an array of clothing, crafts, bootleg watches, designer bags and DVDs.

After exploring the market, take Via Porta di Castro running west from Piazza Ballarò. Nearing the end of the street, turn left along Via Generale Cadorna and first right into Vicolo San Mercurio. Stop for a drink or meal at the peaceful **Villa San Giovanni degli Eremiti**, see ➋.

SAN GIOVANNI DEGLI EREMITI

At the end of the street cross the busy Via dei Benedettini for **San Giovanni degli Eremiti** ➑ (St John of the Hermits; Mon–Sat 9am–7pm, Sun & Mon 9am–1.30pm; charge), distinctive for its five red cupolas. This ruined Benedictine abbey lies amid gardens of orange and mandarin trees, hibiscus, jasmine and acanthus. Built in 1132, it incorporates a Norman-Arab church, with a simple unadorned interior, the hall of an earlier mosque and delightful Norman cloisters planted with palms and kumquat trees.

PALAZZO DEI NORMANNI

Just north of San Giovanni degli Eremiti lies the Palazzo Reale, the eclectic royal palace, or the **Palazzo dei Normanni** ➒, as it is generally known. Centre of power since Byzantine times, it is now seat of the Sicilian Parliament. The Christians razed the Roman fort, the Arabs imposed a Moorish castle, remod-

Lively Ballarò market

elled by the Normans and later embellished by the Spanish. Under both the Arabs and Normans, the palace was one of the most splendid courts in Europe.

Cappella Palatina

Little of the Arab-Norman palace remains, but one exquisite remnant is the **Cappella Palatina** ❿ (Palatine Chapel; Mon–Sat 8.15am–5.40pm, Sun 8.15am–1pm but no visit from 9.45am–11am when religious celebrations take place; charge), the royal chapel built for Roger II between 1130 and 1140 and one of the great highlights of a visit to Sicily.

The interior, akin to a jewel–encrusted casket, displays glittering mosaics on every surface. The oldest are those in the cupola and apse, designed to recall the life of Roger II as well as depict biblical scenes. **Christ Pantocrator** (Christ the All-Powerful), encircled by angels and saints, glimmers in the cupola. The chapel represents the fusion of Byzantine, Arab, Norman and Sicilian civilisations and harmoniously combines the three different styles. Greek, Latin and Kurif (early Arabic) script adorns the walls and capitals, a reminder of the languages of the Norman court. Arab craftsmen created the exquisitely carved and painted **coffered ceiling**, a panoply of Middle Eastern splendour. The Normans commissioned them to portray paradise; the Arabs gleefully conjured up naked maidens, which the rather prudish Normans clothed

and crowned with haloes. Still, the roof remains a paradise of the senses: Persian octagonal stars meet Islamic stalactites. Hunters and revellers languish amidst palm trees entwined with dancers and female musicians; beyond, additional female musicians float into an *Arabian Nights* fantasy.

Royal Apartments

A marble staircase leads from the chapel to the **Royal Apartments**, once home to Spanish viceroys. As the seat of the **Sicilian Regional Parliament**, the visiting hours are limited (Fri–Mon only 8.15am–5.40pm, Sun 8.15am–1pm; www.fondazionefedericosecondo.it; guided tours 20 mins; charge). Most of the apartments were decorated in the 19th century and are rather dull, but it is worth a visit if only for the splendid **Sala di Re Ruggero** (King Roger's Salon), adorned with exotic 12th-century mosaics depicting lions, deer and peacocks set among palms and citrus trees.

From the ground floor of the palace you can descend underground to see the remains of the ancient **Phoenician-Roman walls** of Palermo, and the frescoed **Sala Duca di Montalto**, the setting for art exhibitions.

CATTEDRALE

Turn left out of the Palazzo dei Normanni and go down Via del Bastione following the bastions for **Piazza della Vittoria** ⓫, with its lawns and lofty

Tranquil cloisters of San Giovanni

palms. The Corso Vittorio Emanuele on the far side will bring you to the **Cattedrale** ⓬ (Mon–Sat 9am–5.30pm, Sun 7am–1pm, 4–7pm; www.cattedrale.palermo.it; cathedral free, charges for Treasury, Crypt and Royal Tombs).

Built in 1185 but not completed until 1801 when the dome was added, the building is a Sicilian hybrid: the 12th-century towers are Norman, the facade and south porch are Gothic, and the interior, after the golden, mostly medieval facade, is coldly neoclassical. The main entrance is a beautiful Gothic porch that includes a column with an inscription from the Koran. The church is a pantheon of the Normans, with six royal tombs on the left of the main entrance. The finest tomb was destined for Roger II, but Frederick II expropriated it. Roger now rots in a humbler tomb while his daughter, Queen Constance, lies in the sarcophagus on the far right. In the 1700s, the Cathedral was used as a solar 'observatory', and also features a bronze line on the floor known as *meridiana*, whose ends mark the positions as at the summer and winter solstices. The cathedral borders **Il Capo**, one of the city's poorest districts and the setting for the Capo market.

For dinner in the vicinity, try the Sicilian specialities at **Trattoria Primavera**, see ❸, along the Corso on Piazza Bologni.

Food and Drink

❶ PIZZERIA BELLINI

Piazza Bellini 6; tel: 091 616 5691; daily noon–midnight; €–€€

Some of the best pizzas in town are served in the arcades of a now defunct theatre on Piazza Bellini. Fish dishes and pasta, for example with sardines and aubergines, are also on offer and it is open all day for drinks. For a table outside or upstairs, overlooking two Moorish churches, book ahead.

❷ VILLA SAN GIOVANNI DEGLI EREMITI

Vicolo S. Mercurio 26; tel: 091 253 1643; daily 9am–midnight; www.villasangiovannideglieremiti.it; €–€€

Close to the eponymous church, the terrace/garden of this family-run restaurant/pizzeria/bar is an oasis away from the fracas. Try their *caponata* with home-made bread, sardines Sicilian-style, grilled fish or meat and ricotta-filled *cannoli*, with a glass of Zibibbo wine.

❸ TRATTORIA PRIMAVERA

Piazza Bologni 4; tel: 091 329 408; L and D Tue–Sat, L Sun; €€

This lively, good-value *trattoria* serves authentic Sicilian fare. Choose from the extensive and colourful spread of antipasti, *pasta con le sarde* (fresh sardines), *pasta con i broccoli* and grilled calamari.

Oratorio di Santa Cita

EASTERN PALERMO

Start the day with sumptuous Baroque oratories, then descend into the centuries-old Vucciria Market and explore the ancient neighbourhood of La Kalsa. Following a visit to Sicily's most engaging art collection, the day ends on Palermo's new seafront, Il Foro Italico.

DISTANCE: 3km (2 miles)
TIME: A full day
START: Oratorio di Santa Cita
END: Villa Giulia
POINTS TO NOTE: Consider booking tickets at Teatro Massimo, www.teatro massimo.it, which has a wonderful programme of opera, ballet and concerts (see page 120). A few safety tips to bear in mind: beware of pickpockets in the market and take care in the backstreets at night.

The restored oratories (Catholic chapels) found at the beginning of the route display exquisite stuccowork by Giacomo Serpotta. In his hands simple square chambers are transformed into theatres of irresistible grace and gaiety. These quiet oratories have surprisingly few visitors and feel off the beaten track.

In the southeast, La Kalsa is one of the most interesting parts of Palermo. In Arab times the emir lived in splendour here and during the Middle Ages it was the home of wealthy merchants. Today it is a picturesque but impoverished quarter, having been badly damaged during World War II. But regeneration is ongoing, especially around the Piazza Marina area.

ORATORIO DI SANTA CITA

Start the day at the **Oratorio di Santa Cita** ❶ (Via Valverde 3; Mon–Sat 9am–6pm, winter 9am–4pm; charge), accessed via a Renaissance loggia with garden. Serpotta's art here is at its most exuberant, with walls literally overflowing with cherubs playing with scrolls, garlands, swags of fruit and military trophies. Spectacular scenes painted on the end wall depict the victory of the Christian fleets over the Turks at the famous Battle of Lepanto (1571).

As Paul Duncan, author of *Sicily*, observes: 'You can nearly hear the chortling, farting and giggling of the putti, the rustling of undergrowth, the crack of a bottom slapped, and the swish of drapery.'

Puppet Theatre display

ORATORIO DEL ROSARIO DI SAN DOMENICO

Turn right at the end of the road, crossing the square for Via Malta and Via Bambinai. The **Oratorio del Rosario di San Domenico** ❷ (Mon–Fri 9am–6pm, winter 9am–4pm; charge) at No 16 is a Baroque jewel, another Serpotta oratory, where merchants worshipped in an interior encrusted with seashells, angels and cello-playing cherubs. The Virtues, with their sweet faces and sensual bodies, were modelled on aristocratic Palermitan ladies.

The altarpiece is a beautiful depiction of the *Madonna of the Rosary* (1628) by Van Dyck.

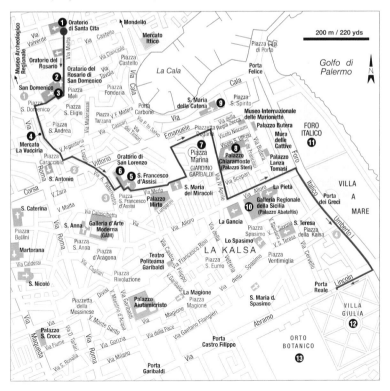

Oratorio ceiling   *La Kalsa*

AROUND SAN DOMENICO

Turn right at the end of the street, past a cluster of jewellers, for **San Domenico** ❸ (Tue–Sun 8.30am–12.30pm; free), a Baroque church with an imposing twin-towered facade overlooking the piazza.

For a break from the Baroque and a spot of retail therapy or sustenance pop into the stylish **Rinascente**, see ❶, on the square.

THE VUCCIRIA MARKET

From Piazza San Domenico follow your nose south down Via Maccheronai through the labyrinthine streets of the ramshackle **Vucciria Market** ❹ (Mercato La Vucciria). Under red awnings, lit by lines of bare light bulbs, stalls display huge barrels of olives, sacks of spices as well as fried aubergines, chickpea or giblet snacks (see page 16).

On Piazza Caracciolo, the fishermen's square, bloody swordfish and tuna steaks glisten on ice blocks alongside boiled octopus and live slithery eels. This is Palermo's oldest market and used to be its largest, but the encroachment of Mafia-controlled modern blocks has reduced it in size and the market now only truly bustles on Saturdays (the Ballarò [see page 32] has taken over as the city's number one market).

For lunch you could grab a *pani cu' la meusa*, boiled beef spleen in a bread roll – a local favourite from market stalls, or

if this is not your scene try the atmospheric **Casa del Brodo**, see ❷, nearby on the main Corso Vittorio Emanuele.

LA KALSA

From **Corso Vittorio Emanuele** turn left and take the third turning on the right, Via A. Paternostro. On the little Piazza S. Francesco d'Assisi the **Antica Focacceria San Francesco**, see ❸, is a Palermitan institution. The Church of **San Francesco d'Assisi** ❺ (Mon–Fri 7–11.30am, 4–6pm, Sun 7am–1pm) opposite has a splendid rose window and portal.

The nearby **Oratorio di San Lorenzo** ❻ (daily 10am–6pm; charge) has another Serpotta interior with lavish stucco decoration depicting the lives of St Francis and St Lawrence. Caravaggio's *Nativity*, featuring both saints, adorned the altar until it was stolen in 1969. Walk down Via Merlo for Piazza Marina.

Piazza Marina

Piazza Marina ❼, the first area in La Kalsa which was renovated, contains the **Giardino Garibaldi** where old boys play dominoes and cards under banyan trees. The piazza is flanked by open-air bars and restaurants, and overlooked by handsome palazzi, including the **Palazzo Chiaramonte** ❽ (on the far side, also known as Palazzo Steri), a Catalan Gothic fortress that was a feudal stronghold before becoming the local seat of the Inquisition in 1598. The palace commands views of Piazza Marina, where

Orto Botanico

heretics and dissenters were burnt. It is now part of Palermo's university, has been restored and is occasionally open for exhibitions. Families will enjoy the **Museo Internazionale delle Marionette Antonio Pasqualino** (Puppet Theatre; Via Butera, on the other side of Palazzo Chiaramonte; www.museomarionettepalermo.it; Mon–Sat 9am–1pm, 2.30–6.30pm; charge), which has an exotic collection of puppets. Entertain-

ing performances are held here from October to April, normally every Tuesday and Friday at 5.30pm (see page 21).

North of the square, the charming Catalan Gothic church of **Santa Maria della Catena** ❾ (daily 10am–6pm; charge) reopened to the public in 2010 after restoration. It was named after the chain *(catena)* that closed the nearby La Cala harbour at night in medieval times. The restored harbour, with a palm-lined promenade, is now full of swish yachts.

Antique treasures

A few blocks away from Santa Cita, the building which houses the Museo Archeologico Regionale Salinas (Piazza Olivella 24; www.regione.sicilia.it/beniculturali/salinas), Palermo's Archaeological Museum, is undergoing major renovation work but should be reopening partially in late 2014. It is housed in a late Renaissance monastery and displays one of the richest collections of Greek and Roman antiquities in Italy.

Most of the treasures come from the Sicilian sites of Tindari, Termini Imerese, Agrigento, Siracusa, Selinunte and Mozia. The highlight are the Classical finds from the temples at Selinunte (see page 57) displayed in the magnificent Sala di Selinunte. Stylised friezes portray Athena protecting Perseus as he battles with Medusa, Hercules slaying dwarves, Hercules and the Cretan Bull, Zeus marrying a frosty Hera and Actaeon attacked by his own dogs.

Galleria Regionale della Sicilia

Take the Via IV Aprile south from the square for the Via Alloro, and turn left for the **Palazzo Abatellis**, home to the revamped **Galleria Regionale della Sicilia** ❿ (Tue–Fri 9am–6pm, Sat and Sun 9am–1pm; charge). The Catalan Gothic mansion and Renaissance loggia make a charming setting for Sicilian paintings and sculpture from the 15th and 16th centuries. The showpiece is the macabre but compelling 15th-century anonymous *Triumph of Death*: a skeletal grim reaper cuts a swathe through the nobles' earthly pleasures. Other great treasures are Francesco Laurana's marble bust of *Eleanor of Aragon*, the Flemish Jan Gossaert's *Malvagna Triptych* (c.1520) and Antonello da Messina's *Annunciation*, a breathtaking portrait of the Virgin surprised at her reading by the Archangel Gabriel. With a short detour, right behind the Galleria Regionale stands the former church and convent of Santa Maria dello Spasimo on Via dello

Palazzo Abatellis fresco   *Foro Italico*

Spasimo, which makes a charming setting for cultural events (see page 120). The complex is open from Tuesday to Sunday 9am–6pm.

The new seafront

Follow Via Alloro east in the direction of the **Foro Italico** ⓫. This was Palermo's grand seafront in the days of the Belle Epoque and a place for both public parade and louche encounters. The area fell into decline until the creation of the promenade. The waterfront now features gardens and pathways, popular with joggers, football-players and sunbathers, and stretches all the way to the gardens of the **Villa Giulia** ⓬ and the delightful **Orto Botanico** ⓭ (Botanical Gardens; daily 9am–8pm, winter until 6pm; charge), a refreshing oasis full of tropical plants and shady walkways.

For a laidback evening with the locals, opt for **Kursaal Kalhesa**, see ➍, located within the old bastions.

Food and Drink

➊ LA RINASCENTE

Via Roma 289; tel: 091 601 7811; daily 11am–midnight; www.larinascente.it; €–€€

The top floor with terrace of this stylish department store has an Obikà mozzarella bar, as well as other eateries. In the evenings cool Palmeritans will sip cocktails while watching the facades on Piazza San Domenico turn from tawny to violet.

➋ CASA DEL BRODO

Corso Vittorio Emanuele 175; tel: 091 321 655; L and D, but closed Sun in summer, Tue in winter; €

This pleasantly old-fashioned restaurant started off in the late 19th century as a soup (*brodo*) kitchen and still remains in the same family. Based on ancient recipes, soup still features on the menu along with other Sicilian fare, such as linguine with sea urchins and *sarde a beccafico* (stuffed sardines).

➌ ANTICA FOCACCERIA SAN FRANCESCO

Via A. Paternostro 58; tel: 091 320 264; www.afsf.it; L and D every day; €

Not to everyone's taste, but it is quaint, boisterous and rough and ready. Recommended by the Slow Food association, this is the place for *trippa* (tripe), *arancine* (fried rice balls) and *panelle* (chickpea fritters). It does also serve 'non-street' food, but that would be missing the point.

➍ KURSAAL KALHESA

Foro Umberto I, 21; tel: 091 616 2282; www.kursaalkalhesa.it; Tue–Fri noon–3pm, 6pm–1.30am, Sat–Sun noon–1.30am; €€

Spend an exotic night out at this special restaurant cum wine bar, bookshop and concert venue in the heart of La Kalsa. Prop up the bar with cool young Palermitans, sip an aperitif or tuck into fusion food in the garden above, where the heady perfume of jasmine fills the air.

The steps to the Duomo

CEFALÙ

Sitting snugly below a majestic headland, Cefalù is a picturesque family-friendly resort boasting a great cathedral, golden sands and a leisurely pace of life. Explore the alleys of the old quarter, climb the Rocca for bird's-eye views – or simply chill out on the beach.

DISTANCE: 3km (2 miles) including La Rocca (1 mile/1.5km without La Rocca)
TIME: A half-day walk
START: Piazza del Duomo
END: Seafront
POINTS TO NOTE: Frequent trains and buses link Cefalù with Palermo (70km [44 miles] away); both take an hour and arrive at the railway station 10 minutes' walk from the centre. By car from Palermo take the A19 and A20 or the more leisurely route along the coastal SS113. You can park along the seafront.

Cefalù is arguably the most charming resort on the Tyrrhenian coast. The medieval port retains its character, helped by a pervasive Arab atmosphere and a compact fishbone design which curls its way to the shore. The town may be a summer tourist trap (try to avoid July and August) but the old quarter, with its narrow cobbled alleys, retains its medieval air. For families in particular, Cefalù makes a welcoming base.

IL DUOMO

Start the morning in one of the outdoor cafés on **Piazza del Duomo**, admiring the twin-towered facade of the Arab-Norman **Duomo** ❶ (daily 8am–6.45pm, 5.30pm off season; free). The cathedral was built in 1131 by Roger II. The king had a sarcophagus made for himself, but he and his tomb are in Palermo Cathedral as he died before the Duomo here was completed. Inside, the austere nave is flanked by Roman columns spanned by slender pointed arches betraying Islamic influence.

Mosaics
The eye is immediately drawn by the simple beauty of the mosaic of **Christ Pantocrator** in the apse, set above the Madonna, archangels and apostles. The All-Powerful's blessing is the standard Orthodox form: two raised fingers symbolise the duality of Christ's spiritual and temporal power, while the other fingers and thumb represent the Trinity. The left hand holds open the Bible with the Greek and Latin text (John 8:12) 'I

Cefalù beach *Duomo fresco*

am the light of the world.' In the purest Byzantine style this is the acknowledged masterpiece of Sicilian mosaic art.

Don't miss the charming cathedral **cloisters** (chiostri; daily 10am–1pm, 3–6pm, 2–4pm off season; charge), to the left of the main entrance, and comprising three rows of elegant twin columns, with finely carved capitals.

THE OLD QUARTER

From the piazza, narrow alleys lead into the old town. Via Mandralisca slopes down to the **Museo Mandralisca ❷**

(daily 9am–7pm, 11pm in summer; charge), a small museum home to Sicily's most enigmatic painting. The Renaissance *Portrait of an Unknown Man* (1465) by the Sicilian master Antonello da Messina is famed for the sitter's supercilious smile and Machiavellian expression. The collection was set up by Baron Mandralisca (1809–64), who discovered the portrait in a Lípari pharmacy.

From here explore the old quarter with its warren of alleyways and some appealing relics. At the end of Via Mandralisca turn left for the **Lavatoio Medievale ❸**, where curved steps lead down

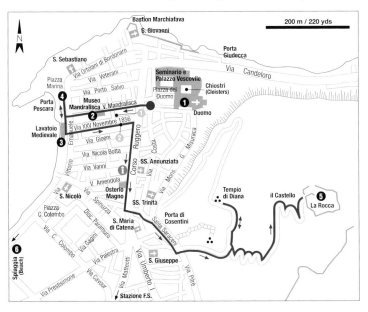

Cefalù skyline

to an arcaded Arab wash-house with cold river water. Take the Via Vittorio Emanuele north to the **Porta Pescara** ❹, the old Arab port used in many films, including *Cinema Paradiso*.

Back towards the cathedral, take Via XXV Novembre 1856, home to two good restaurants: **La Brace**, see ❶, and **Le Chat Noir**, see ❷. Or head to **Corso Ruggero**, the medieval main street, and buy a picnic to enjoy at La Rocca or the beach.

LA ROCCA

Above the medieval town and on the site of the original Arab town, **La Rocca** ❺ (May–Sept 9am–7pm, Oct–Apr 9am–4.30pm, closed in inclement weather; free) affords sweeping views over Cefalù and the sea. For the pathway up, head south along Corso Ruggero, then left along Vicolo Saraceni following the signs for Tempio di Diana. Allow two hours for the round trip up to the top (in summer it can be a sweltering slog). The Salita Saraceno climbs up three tiers of city walls to the restored fortifications of the crumbling stone castle, revealing traces of a pool, fountain, cistern and prison. The most conspicuous structure, which you come to after a 20-minute climb, is the so-called **Tempio di Diana**, circa 4th century BC.

If La Rocca sounds too strenuous, head for the **beach** ❻, one of the best in Sicily and hugely popular in summer. Parasols and deckchairs can be rented from May to September.

PARCO REGIONALE DELLE MADONIE

Cefalù is the gateway to the delightful Madonie mountains (www.parcodellemadonie.it). Buses run from Cefalù but to explore the winding roads and medieval villages you need a car. The mountains are popular with hikers, but be aware that some of the paths are very demanding and good maps are hard to come by. Information can be found at the park offices in Cefalù (Corso Ruggero 116) and Castelbueno.

Food and Drink

❶ LA BRACE

Via XXV Novembre 1856, 10; tel: 0921 423 570; D only Tue–Sun; www.ristorantelabrace.com; €–€€
This welcoming restaurant is excellent value and hugely popular. The menu offers specialities such as stuffed aubergines and Sicilian stuffed meatballs, and a good choice of desserts. Book ahead.

❷ LE CHAT NOIR

Via XXV Novembre 1856, 17; tel: 0921 420 697; L and D Thur–Tue; www.ristorantelechatnoir.com; €€
Despite the name, this family-run restaurant is dedicated to classic Sicilian dishes such as *caponata* or *involtini ri pisci spade* (swordfish filled with aubergine and cheese and topped with breadcrumbs).

Monreale cloisters

MONREALE, SEGESTA AND ZÍNGARO PARK

Leave behind the bustle of Palermo for the sumptuous Arab-Norman cathedral of Monreale and the evocative temple of Segesta. Discover the coastal paths of the Zíngaro Nature Reserve, then feast on fresh fish at Castellammare del Golfo.

DISTANCE: 106km (66 miles) plus walk in Zíngaro Nature Reserve
TIME: A full day
START: Palermo
END: Castellammare del Golfo (or Palermo)
POINTS TO NOTE: Wear appropriate dress for Monreale Cathedral – no short shorts or bare shoulders. Monreale is expensive for eating out and Segesta is a lovely spot for a picnic. Take swimming gear and walking shoes for Zíngaro Nature Reserve. The beaches are best avoided in midsummer.

Monreale Cathedral is the apogee of Arab-Norman artistic achievement and one of the wonders of the medieval world. According to a Sicilian proverb, *'He who goes to Palermo without seeing Monreale leaves a donkey and comes back an ass.'* The cathedral was the creation of the Norman King William II, who was known as William the Bad merely because he was slightly less popular than William the Good. From Monreale,

the route heads southwest to the finely preserved Greek temple of Segesta, another cultural highlight, in a glorious isolated setting. After a heady morning's sightseeing the afternoon is spent walking or chilling out on the north coast.

MONREALE

Monreale ❶ is 8km (5 miles) from Palermo. From Piazza Independenza, just west of Palazzo dei Normanni, take the Corso Calatafimi and follow the SS186 for Monreale. Park in one of the signed car parks rather than the streets of the old town. There are no major sights other than the cathedral, but Monreale is an attractive little town for strolling, with narrow alleys, Baroque churches and an abundance of bars, restaurants and souvenir shops.

Cathedral facade

Set high above the Conca d'Oro valley and Palermo, the **cathedral** (Tue–Sat 9am–1pm, 2.30–6.30pm, Sun 9–12am, 2.30–6.30pm; cathedral free, charge to treasury and terraces, north

The cathedral's lofty interior

transept, Museo Diocesano and cloisters; www.cattedraledimonreale.it) was completed in just 10 years. Before entering, take time to look at the **Romanesque portal**, its delicate design inspired by Byzantine inlaid ivory, and the main **bronze door**, adorned with lions and griffins – royal motifs echoed by the Norman throne inside. The **apses** (seen from Via del Arcivescovado) are the most opulent in Sicily, with interlacing arches of limestone and lava, as delicate as wood.

Cathedral interior
Inside, the shimmering tapestry of mosaics is unequalled in Europe. Scholars dispute whether the **mosaics** are wholly Byzantine, finished by 1100, or completed by Venetians before 1250. Given Sicily's mongrel inheritance, it seems probable that they are a fusion of all the invading cultures. Islamic semi-lancet windows and arabesque decoration sit easily with Romanesque columns, marble details and Byzantine backgrounds.

On entry the eye is drawn to the imposing half-length figure of Christ Pantocrator in the central apse, with the enthroned Virgin and Child with angels and apostles below, and lower still, figures of saints. Above the arcade in the nave the luminous mosaics start with the **Creation sequence**. The loveliest of these 42 panels depict the creation of light, the world, the stars, fish and fowl. The Garden of Eden panels enshrine a Palermitan paradise, an orchard of exquisite fruit trees, flowers and exotic birds. Here, a matchmaking God presents a perky Eve to a sleepy Adam.

The Norman kings ruled by divine right, a message proclaimed throughout their cathedrals. Above the royal throne is a mosaic of **Christ crowning William II**, a tribute to a Christian king whose world view embraced concubines, eunuchs and black slaves. In the nearby side chapel William is buried in an elaborate marble sarcophagus.

Tower, terrace and cloisters
In the south of the nave, climb the **tower** (charge) for fine valley and sea views, and from the **terrace** look down onto the splendid **Chiostro dei Bened-**

Monreale Mafia

Perched on a hill, Monreale enjoys fine views and after frenetic Palermo exudes tranquillity. Yet the town is home to the largest Carabinieri (police) barracks in Sicily, built after the Mafia murdered local officers in 1983–4. In 1996 the Archbishop of Monreale was himself investigated for Mafia collusion, extortion and fraud. Although perfectly safe, this touristy little town is reputed still to be a Mafia stronghold. From Monreale, rural roads lead south to the Mafia heartland of gulleys and mountain lairs. Nurtured by the mythology of banditry and the wartime cult of Salvatore Giuliano, Sicily's Robin Hood, the region remains insular.

Cathedral statuary   *Cathedral guided tour*

ettini (Benedictine Cloisters), surrounding a courtyard garden. For a closer look you can enter Piazza Gugliemo (Tue–Sat 9am–7pm, Sun and Mon 9am–1.30pm; charge).

The Romanesque cloisters not only express William's great love of Islamic art but also reflect the cosmopolitan nature of the Norman court. Craftsmen from Provence, Venice, Pisa, Greece, Africa, Persia and elsewhere in Asia all worked on Monreale. Not that the Normans were un-Christian: one sculpted pillar depicts William presenting the cathedral to the Virgin. Every second pair of white marble columns has a vivid zigzag mosaic spiralling up the shaft. A Provençal sophistication is suggested by the columns; by contrast, the Moorish mood is sensuous, evoked by rich mosaic inlays and arabesque carvings. The marble sculptures in the cloisters echo the mosaics but with a personal or secular note, from a mason's signature to an animated picture of tree-planting and pig-killing. A Moorish corner is enhanced by a loggia and a sensuous, slightly phallic fountain. Shaped like a palm–tree trunk, the shaft is crowned by lions' heads, as in Granada's Alhambra.

If lunch can't wait, a good option is **Taverna del Pavone**, see ❶.

SEGESTA

From Monreale come down the hill, follow the SS186 towards Partinico, then north of the town join the A29 autostrada in the Trápani direction. Exit at Segesta. The journey takes about an hour.

Segesta ❷ (daily 9am–1 hour before sunset; charge) is arguably the most eloquent of all Classical sites in Sicily. The temple and theatre, dating from the 5th and 3rd centuries BC respectively, stand on separate hilltops overlooking rolling countryside and sea – still wonderfully empty and isolated, despite the motorway.

The ancient settlement of Egesta (today's Segesta) is thought to have been founded in the 12th century BC by the Elymians, a race who occupied much of northwestern Sicily, but about whom little is known. The settlers had to switch allegiance frequently between Carthaginians and Greeks to ensure survival. They destroyed Greek Selinunte in 409 BC, but a century later, in 307 BC, Agathocles, tyrant of Siracusa, sacked Egesta, killing nearly 10,000 inhabitants and selling others into slavery.

Although one of the best-preserved of Italy's Doric temples, Segesta's **Temple** was never completed. Apart from no roof, the bosses, used for hauling up the stones into position, remain on the steps, the columns are unfluted and there are gaps in the bases of the columns. But it is no less lovely for that.

Take the shuttle bus to the **Teatro** on Monte Barbaro 4km (2.5 miles) away. In spring the hills are a riot of wild flowers and this makes a lovely walk. Excavations on Monte Barbaro are ongoing. The Arabs and Normans settled here

The theatre at Segesta

and there are ruins of an ancient castle and church, but the main attraction is the well-restored Greek theatre cut out of the side of the mountain. With its views of the Golfo di Castellammare, it's a fine backdrop for Greek plays in summer.

SCOPELLO

Return to the A29, direction Palermo, and exit at Castellammare del Golfo. Follow the coast road northwest following signs for **Scopello** ❸, a picturesque rustic hamlet which grew up around a 17th-century farmstead. Enjoy a drink in the main piazza, try the pastries at

Bar/Pasticceria Scopello or a meal at **La Tavernetta**, see ❷. Just east of Scopello, the Tonnara di Scopello (charge) is an old scenic tuna fishery on an irresistible little cove with sparkling blue waters. The fishery has been restored and part of it is now a B&B. Apart from peak season when Scopello is seething with visitors, this is an idyllic place for a dip.

ZÍNGARO NATURE RESERVE

The **Riserva Naturale dello Zíngaro** ❹ (daily Apr–Oct 7am–8pm, Nov–Mar 8am–4pm; charge), sandwiched between mountains and sea, embraces

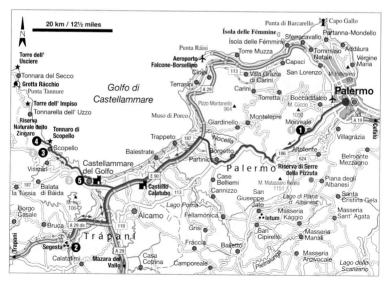

Castellamare beach   *Castellamare harbour*

a 7km (4.3-mile) stretch of gorgeous unspoilt coastline. The path hugs the coast, skirting secret coves, idyllic bays and rocky headlands, but there are also trails inland. The reserve is rich in flora, with yellow euphorbia, palms and carobs; it's also a haunt of buzzards, falcons and the rare Bonelli eagle. Access (on foot only) is a 2km (1.25-mile) drive from Scopello. The coastal path (Sentiero Basso) is well signed but facilities are scant.

The park could occupy an entire day, but if you're considering a short walk and a dip, take the path to Cala Capreria, a lovely cove with a small natural history museum, or it's another 20 minutes to Cala del Varo.

CASTELLAMMARE DEL GOLFO

Head for **Castellammare del Golfo** ❺ in the early evening. Set on the eponymous gulf, near good beaches, this is an overgrown fishing village with a charming harbour below a squat Saracen castle, and fine views across the gulf. Dine at one of the fish restaurants at the harbour. At **La Cambusa**, see ❸, you pay a little bit extra for harbour views, but it's a lovely spot to sit outside (or behind large glass windows) and watch the world go by. Sitting here, it's strange to think that Castellammare was once a notorious Mafia haunt.

Food and Drink

❶ TAVERNA DEL PAVONE
Vicolo Pensato 18, Monreale; tel: 091 640 6414; www.tavernadelpavone.eu; L and D daily; €€–€€€
This cosy, welcoming inn offers traditional dishes such as *caponata* (fried aubergines with tomato, pine nuts and olives), *cacciocavallo* cheese and sardines, Sicilian style.

❷ LA TAVERNETTA
Via Armando Diaz 3, Scopello; tel: 0924 541 129; www.albergolatavernetta.it; D daily (tel in advance for lunch); closed Nov–Mar €–€€

Try the home-made pasta and Sicilian specialities at this charming little hotel restaurant. It is family-run, very friendly and has garden and sea views from the restaurant terrace. Not always open for lunch.

❸ LA CAMBUSA
Via Don Luigi Zangara 67; Castellamarre del Golfo; tel: 0924 30155 and 334 6002594. Closed from Christmas to end of January; www.ristorante-lacambusa.it; noon–11pm; €€
Watch the fishing boats and the local *passeggiata* as you tuck into all things fishy at this popular harbourfront restaurant. An extensive choice includes mussel soup, smoked tuna, grilled squid and fish couscous and it's open all day for meals.

Trápani beach

TRÁPANI AND ERICE

A lively port since Phoenician times, Trápani now has an elegant centre with revamped churches, palaces and seafront. On a mountain high above, exquisite Erice is the island's moodiest medieval town: lovely in any season, whether swathed in winter mists or a carpet of spring flowers.

DISTANCE: Walk in Trápani: 3.5km (2 miles); Trápani centre to Erice 12km (7.5 miles) by car, bus or cable car
TIME: A full day
START: Trápani centre
END: Erice
POINTS TO NOTE: For buses to Trápani from Palermo go to www.segesta.it, for trains www.trenitalia.it. The train and bus stations are about a 15-minute walk from the old centre. By car from Palermo take the A29 motorway. Avoid parking in the old centre. Trápani has its own airport at Birgi, 16km (10 miles) south of town with a bus service to City Terminal at Trápani. The Trápani/Erice cable car (www.funiviaerice.it) is closed in winter, on Mondays all year and when the weather is inclement. Pedestrians should consider purchasing the Trápani Welcome Card (www.trapaniwelcome. it), which lasts three days and allows unlimited travel on public transport, one return journey on the cable car to Erice, 50 percent off Castello Venere and many discounts on other attractions.

Squeezed onto a narrow promontory on the west coast, Trápani was once the centre of trade for coral, tuna and salt with the Levant, Carthage and Venice. Today it is a fishing and ferry port, as well as an arrival point for budget airlines from Europe (and Italy).

Until recently Trápani was seen as a workaday city in which to kill time before the next ferry to the Egadi Islands. But it has changed: Baroque churches have been restored, the main Corso Vittorio Emanuele partially pedestrianised and the dodgy fishing quarter converted into a seafront promenade. Drivers in Trápani should always check the street-cleaning timetable when parking along the harbour road, as the car will be towed away if it's parked there during the official street-cleaning times – even if you've paid for the parking fee.

The sprawling modern outskirts are hardly welcoming and there are no great sites, but Trápani is certainly worth a visit for the old quarter, the salty port and the seafood eateries with their delicious fish couscous *alla trapanese* made with sea

Fishing boats in Trápani harbour

bass, sea bream, red mullet, grouper, mussels, clams and prawns, and a sprinkling of chilli.

A world apart from Trápani, Erice makes a more peaceful base for exploring – and staying. Perched 750m (2,500ft) above the coast on a windswept isolated mountain, it is a small fortified medieval town. The sea views are staggering, and on a clear day you can spot the Egadi Islands and, according to the locals, even Cape Bon in Tunisia.

The city was founded by the Elymians, the mysterious settlers of Segesta who built a richly decorated temple dedicated to the fertility goddess known as Astarte (Aphrodite to the Greeks and Venus to the Romans). The mountain was much fought over, particularly by the Romans and Carthaginians. The Arabs called it *Gebel-Hamed*, Mohammed's Mountain, and Count Roger, who had visions of St Julian while attacking the town, renamed it Monte San Giuliano.

TRÁPANI

The centre

The old town has an easy charm, with its 11th-century Spanish fortifications matched by a regenerated seafront. Set on a narrow curving promontory, it was formerly named Drepanon, the ancient Greek for sickle. This is where most of the sights are clustered. If you're feeling peckish, pop into **Angelino**, see ❶.

Head inland along the elegant **Via Torrearsa**, the main shopping street, then west along **Corso Vittorio Emanuele**, which cuts through the 'sickle' and at its eastern end closes with a grand Baroque flourish at **Palazzo Sen-**

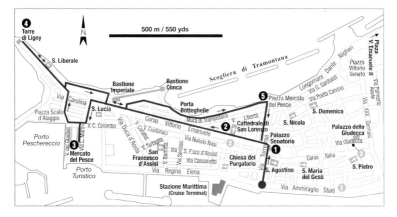

Cloisters in Trápani

atorio **❶**, the town hall. The Corso is flanked by fine balconied palaces and churches, including the imposing **Cattedrale di San Lorenzo ❷** (daily 8am–4pm; free).

Follow the road to the end of the promontory, diverting slightly south for the new **Mercato del Pesce ❸** (Fish Market) next to the **fishing port**. Here you can buy cheese, bunches of oregano, *bottarga* (dried tuna roe), as well as fresh fish.

At the tip of the promontory, the **Torre di Ligny ❹** (Mon–Sat 10am–12.30, 4–6.30pm [7.30pm in midsummer]; charge) is a squat Spanish fortress built in 1671, now restored and housing a small collection of archaeological finds hauled from the seabed. Softly illuminated, the tower now makes a romantic evening stroll.

Return to the centre via the ancient Spanish bastions on the north side of the promontory – there are steps from Porta Botteghelle for good views of the bay and fishermen's cottages. The seawalls here lead along to **Piazza Mercato del Pesce ❺**, site of the former fish market.

For lunch head back to Corso Vittorio Emanuele, taking Via Torrearsa south, and try the delicious home-made fare at **La Tavernetta Ai Lumi**,

see **❷**, at No. 75; or try **Cantina Siciliana**, see **❸**, the oldest *osteria* in the city, in the heart of the faded Jewish quarter to the east.

The modern town

The city's main monument, the **Santuario dell'Annunziata ❻** (Via Conte Pepoli; daily 7am–noon, 4–7pm; free) lies in modern Trápani, about 3km (2 miles) east of the old town. Drive east along the main Via G. B. Fardella and bear right at Via Pepoli, or take bus No. 25 or 30 from Piazza Vittorio Emanuele.

The Carmelite church, founded in 1315 but rebuilt in 1760, has a rococo nave and a cluster of exotic domed chapels. Behind the high altar is the lavish **Cappella della Madonna**, with the revered statue of the Madonna di Trápani by Nino Pisano, crowned in jewels. This venerated Madonna is credited with miraculous powers.

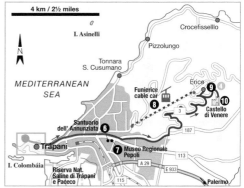

Erice castle   *Pasticceria Maria Grammatico*

The **Museo Regionale Pepoli** ❼ (Mon−Sat 9am−1.30pm, 2−7.30pm, Sun 9am−12.30pm; charge), arranged around the beautiful cloister of the former convent adjoining the cathedral, is the city's eclectic museum of regional sculpture, paintings and crafts.

ERICE

The writer Carlo Levi called Erice 'the Assisi of the south, full of churches, convents, silent streets and mythological memories'. But this is no sanctuary, especially in summer. Orphanages and convents have been converted into cute craft shops or restaurants and, in midsummer, music festivals are held in the cobbled squares.

The town lies some 10km (6 miles) northeast of Trápani. If driving, take the main Via G.B. Fardella, and follow the signs all the way up to Erice. Buses depart frequently from City Terminal and the bus station at Piazza Montalto, taking the best part of an hour; the views are lovely, but better still is the **Funierice cable car** ❽ (mid-March to second week of Jan Tue−Fri 7.50am−8pm, Sat 10am−midnight, Sun 10am−8pm; www.funiviaerice. it), which takes just 12 minutes and affords truly wonderful views of saltpans, mountains, sea and islands. Unfortunately it's rather inconveniently located, at the junction of Via Capua and the SP31 (the Trápani to Erice road).

The centre

Buses, cars and the cable car all arrive by the entrance to **Erice** ❾, the Norman **Porta Trápani**. Beyond the gate lies the **Duomo** (also called Chiesa Madre; daily 9.30am−12.30pm, 3−6pm; charge), the largest of Erice's 10 churches and founded by Frederick II; climb the campanile, Torre di Re Federico II (charge), for fabulous views.

Exploring the streets of the medieval town you will invariably spy sweet cakes and pastries. According to legend, Erice lived off *dolci ericini* made by nuns, and **Maria Grammatico**, see ❹, claims the title of the best bakery in Sicily. Those with a less sweet tooth may prefer **Monte San Giuliano** (see page 113), a restaurant just off the main street.

> ## Bitter almonds
>
> In the 1950s Maria Grammatico, who owns the famous Pasticceria Maria Grammatico in Erice, was sent to an orphanage run by nuns. Her father had died of a heart attack and her mother, carrying a sixth child, could not cope alone with such a large family. Life was tough at the orphanage, but it was here that Maria Grammatico learnt to make the sweets and almond pastries for which she is now famed. Her melancholic girlhood recollections are recounted in her autobiography, *Bitter Almonds*, co-authored with Mary Taylor Simeti.

View from Castello di Venere

Castello di Venere

Dominating the rocky outcrop at the top of the town lie the ruins of the **Castello di Venere** ⑩ (Castle of Venus, Apr–Sept 9am–sunset; Oct–Mar 10am–sunset, closed Mon). The castle was constructed during the 12th century on the site of the fabled Tempio di Venere, with blocks from the pagan temple being used for the crenellated Norman walls.

From here there are staggering views, though if you come off season it may be shrouded in mist. Below the castle are the **Giardino del Balio** (public gardens), with an ivy-clad 15th-century tower and more glorious views from the garden terraces. Below stretch wooded groves and vineyards, and a tapestry of saltpans and sea out to the Egadi Islands and as far as Cape Bon in Tunisia.

Food and Drink

① ANGELINO

Via Ammiraglio Staiti 87, Trápani; tel: 0923 26922; www.angelino.it; Tue–Sun 7am–midnight; €

This hugely popular café serves a range of reasonably priced dishes as well as irresistible cakes and pastries. Do as the Sicilians and tuck into the delicious *arancine* (fried rice balls with chopped meat and peas).

② AI LUMI

Corso Vittorio Emanuele 75, Trápani; tel: 0923 540 922; www.ailumi.it; L and D Wed–Mon; closed one month Jan/Feb; €€

Converted from the stables of an old palazzo, this is an atmospheric spot favoured by the fashionable young locals. The cuisine here is traditional Sicilian: succulent steaks, roast lamb and braised rabbit – also very fresh fish and seafood.

③ CANTINA SICILIANA

Via Giudecca 36, Trápani; tel: 0923 28673; www.cantinasiciliana.it; L and D daily, closed Wed from Oct–Mar; €€

This family-run restaurant is renowned for authentic Trapanese and Sicilian fare: *cuscus alla trapanese*, with fried calamari, *busiate al pesto trapanese* (home-made pasta with basil, garlic, almonds and tomato pesto), swordfish with tomatoes, capers and almonds, and tuna in various forms.

④ PASTICCERIA MARIA GRAMMATICO

Via Vittorio Emanuele 14, Erice; tel: 0923 869 390; www.mariagrammatico.it; daily 7am–10pm, closed Tue in winter; €

This is Sicily's most famous *pasticceria*. Try the *cannoli*, marzipan fruits, *dolci di badia* (almond cakes), *mustaccioli* (chocolate and almond biscuits) – to name a few. Maria Grammatico also own the Caffè Maria with a panoramic terrace down the road at No. 4 and Antica Pasticceria del Convento in Piazzetta San Domenico.

Saltplans at Nubia

ALONG THE AFRICAN COAST

*This seafaring region represents a swathe of ancient Sicily, from **Phoenician** Mozia to Greek Selinunte and Arab Mazara del Vallo. At Marsala you can taste the eponymous wine and visit a **Punic ship**.*

DISTANCE: 88km (55 miles)
TIME: A full day
START: Trápani
END: Selinunte
POINTS TO NOTE: Set off early to allow plenty of time for Selinunte – or miss out Marsala or Mazara del Vallo. For information on ferries to Mozia, see www.mozialine.com or www.arinie pugliese.com.

The west coast of Sicily is often known as the African coast because it is closer to Tunisia than to mainland Italy, and its early settlers were Arabs from North Africa. The landscape spans dazzling saltpans, Marsala vineyards and coastal nature reserves.

THE SALT ROAD (TRÁPANI TO MARSALA)

Follow the narrow coastal road south of Trápani (SP21), where mountains of salt are signs of an industry that dates from antiquity. The **Museo del Sale** ❶

(Salt Museum, Núbia, 6.5km (4 miles) south of Trápani; daily 9.30am–7pm; charge, www.museodelsale.it) demonstrates salt production, and has an inviting *trattoria*.

Rejoin the coast road and follow brown signs for *Imbarco per Mozia* (also signed Mothia and Motya). This ancient Phoenician settlement lies on the tiny island of San Pantaleo, one of the **Isole dello Stagnone** ❷, a marshy trio of lagoon islands and now a nature reserve, home to wild ducks, pink flamingos, avocets and African cranes. From the Ettore e Infersa saltworks, small ferries chug across to San Pantaleo. A finely restored salt windmill here sells pots of orange, coriander or juniper-flavoured salt. Trápani salt is said to be the best in Italy.

MOZIA

Sicily's chief Punic site, **Mozia** ❸ or Motya as it was known, was a colony set within a ring of ramparts and towers. During the 8th century BC the Phoenicians colonised the west coast, from

Marsala Cathedral

Marsala to Palermo and Solunto, and Motya was the first Sicilian outpost of this naval and trading empire. In 398 BC Dionysius I, tyrant of Siracusa, besieged the town.

Motya was bought in the early 1900s by Joseph Whitaker, a wealthy merchant who discovered Phoenician remains while inspecting vines on the island. The **Museo Whitaker** (Mon–Sat 9am–2pm; charge) displays Punic and Greek pottery, hundreds of burial urns, carved *stelae* and jewellery. The prize piece is a Greek statue from the early 5th century BC of a sinuous youth, *The Man in a Tunic*. The ruins of Motya are still only partially excavated but you can still see remains of the city walls, the Punic dry dock and the **Tophet**, a sacrificial site where the Phoenicians worshipped sun, moon and fertility deities. The charred offerings of animals and jars containing burnt babies, sacrificed to the gods, were unearthed. Close to the museum the **Casa dei Mosaici** has black and white pebble floor mosaics of exotic animals.

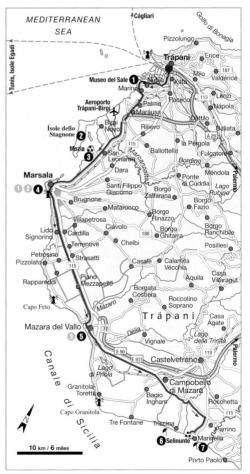

Garibaldi Gate, Marsala   *Fishmonger in Mazara*

MARSALA

Continue on the coast road to **Marsala ④** (12km/7.5 miles), famous for dessert wine (see box). Set on Sicily's most westerly cape, Marsala was originally a Carthaginian port called Lilybaeum, and derived its present name from the Arabic Mars-al-Allah, 'the port of God'. In the later Middle Ages it became the frequent victim of African-based pirate raids, and Trápani took over as the major trading port – except for wine.

Wine apart, Marsala is a pleasant town of Baroque buildings, lending itself to a leisurely stroll, a seafood meal and a glass or two of the local tipple. Sample a fine Marsala in one of the *enoteche* (wine bars) in Via Garibaldi such as **La Sirena Ubriaca**, see ❶, or try a glass over a fish grill at nearby **Trattoria Garibaldi**, see ❷. On 11 May 1860, Garibaldi, along with his Redshirts, landed at Marsala, freeing the island of the Bourbon regime and setting the stage for the Unification of Italy. Throughout Marsala you can see plaques to the famous freedom fighter.

Archaeological Park of Lilybaeum

Capo Boeo, the western tip of Sicily, is the city's archaeological zone. On the seafront, the **Museo Archeologico** (tel: 0923 952 535; Tue–Sun 9am–7pm, Mon 9.30am–1pm; charge) displays ancient ruins from the city and a reconstructed 35m (115ft) long Punic warship

discovered by an English archaeologist in 1971 in the Stagnone lagoon, and believed to have sunk off the Egadi Islands during the First Punic War in 241 BC. It doesn't look much, but it's the only surviving Punic warship and has provided invaluable information on life aboard in that era.

The museum gives access to the **Insula Romana**, part of a Roman villa (guided tours 9.30am, 11.30am, 3.30pm and 5.30pm Mar–Oct). The newly accessible **Ipogeo di Crispia Salvia** (Sat only 9am–1pm, booked through Museo Archeologico) reveals a subterranean chamber with fresco fragments of funerary banqueting scenes.

Marsala wine

In 1773 English merchant John Woodhouse shipped 60 oak barrels of rich golden Marsala wine to England, having added a dose of alcohol to ensure it would survive the long journey. The wine was an instant success in England and was soon stocked instead of port by the British navy. Marsala later lost its reputation and was regarded as a cheap sweet liqueur, confined to cooking. Recent years, however, have seen a renaissance in quality, with producers making dry, smooth, amber dessert wines, aged in oak barrels and known as Vergine or Riserva. The market leader is Florio (Via Vincenzo Florio 1, tel 0923 78111), where you can taste all varieties.

MAZARA DEL VALLO

Take the SS115 24km (15 miles) to **Mazara del Vallo ❺**, passing by cube-shaped North African houses and miles of modern sprawl. Mazara may be of Phoenician origin but Arab influences predominate, from the Tunisian trawlermen to the Arab music and shisha pipes. However, the **Kasbah**, with its maze of backstreets, has been newly gentrified with freshly painted houses and ceramic plaques and murals. The town has a long and pleasant tree-shaded seafront, with marina and beach, and a centre of fine churches.

The evocative **Norman Arch**, near the seafront, is all that remains of Count Roger's castle. Across the palm-filled park lies the **Cattedrale** (Piazza della Repubblica; free, irregular hours), rebuilt in the 17th century but retaining Norman apses. From the square, Via XX Settembre takes you to the **Museo del Satiro** (Satyr Museum; daily 9am–7pm; charge), which displays a 4th-century BC bronze satyr recovered from the local seabed in 1997–8.

You could try lunch at **Alla Kasbah** (see page 114), or sample fabulous fish at **Del Pescatore**, see ❶, as you exit town on the SS115.

SELINUNTE

Follow the SS115 east, turning off to Campobello and head for **Selinunte ❻**. Founded by colonists in 628 BC, it took its name from *selinon*, the Greek for wild celery which grew here in abundance. By the 5th century BC it had become a prosperous city with over 100,000 inhabitants, great temples and two harbours. Inevitably the colony became embroiled in the battle between Athens and Phoenician Carthage and was sacked by Carthage in a nine-day siege in 409 BC. The citizens resettled in Marsala (Lilybaeum) and the site was abandoned.

Parco Archeologico

Selinunte's grace lies in its splendid isolated setting by the sea. The **Parco Archeologico** (9am–one hour before sunset; charge) consists of four zones: the acropolis overlooking the sea, the ancient city on the hillside, the sanctu-

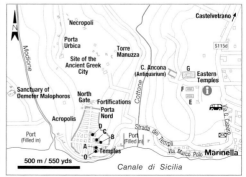

Temple ruins at Selinunte

ary of Malophorus, dedicated to Demeter, goddess of fertility, and the imposing eastern temples that visitors flock to see.

The site is huge, and a guidebook on sale is useful for deciphering the complex. Bikes can be rented, and an electric train covers part of the park.

The temples

Since temple attributions are uncertain, they are identified, rather prosaically, with letters of the alphabet.

Begin with the **main temples** (E, F and G) on the eastern hill. Dating 480–460 BC and partly reconstructed in 1958, **Temple E**, possibly dedicated to Hera (Juno) and in pure Doric style, is the most dramatic and complete of the temples. **Temple F**, in ruins, is dedicated perhaps to Athena, while **Temple G** is a vast heap of ruins with one restored column rising from the rubble. It was one of the largest temples of Classical antiquity.

From here stroll along the Strada dei Templi to the **Acropolis**, with the remains of the oldest temples (**A, B, C, D and O**) and reconstructed walls. Nearest the sea are the elusive **Temples O and A** (480–470 BC).

The more conspicuous **Temple C**, with 14 standing columns and splendid sea views, is the oldest of the other three temples. The lovely metopes which embellished this and other temples are housed in Palermo's Archaeological Museum.

North of the acropolis are great views of the ancient city and, on either side, the necropolis – quarters yet to be explored.

Marinella

A walk along the sandy beach of neighbouring **Marinella** makes a pleasant end to the day. The seafront at this modern resort is lined with lively seafood restaurants (see page 114).

Food and Drink

1 LA SIRENA UBRIACA

Via Garibaldi 39, Marsala; tel: 328 105 3522; daily 10am–10pm or later; €

A good spot to sample Marsala and other wines, accompanied by *crostini*, olives and dips. The hosts of this small enoteca are multilingual and will guide you through the different Marsalas – it's not called the Drunken Mermaid for nothing.

2 TRATTORIA GARIBALDI

Piazza dell'Addolorata 35, Marsala; tel: 0923 953 006; L & D Mon–Fri, D Sat, L Sun; €€

This popular trattoria in the centre offers a fine spread of seafood and vegetable antipasti, *pasta con le sarde* (sardines), fish couscous or simply grilled fish – or meat.

3 DEL PESCATORE

Via Castelvetrano 191, Mazara del Vallo; tel: 0923 947 580; L and D Tue–Sun; €€€

Enjoy the very freshest of fish and seafood in a formal but quite simple setting. There are no menus here – just choose your fish, have it weighed and then cooked to perfection by the chef behind the glass panel.

VALLEY OF THE TEMPLES, AGRIGENTO

Dramatic ruins of one of the ancient world's greatest cities face the sea on the south coast of Sicily. The Doric temples in the Valle dei Templi rival the finest ancient ruins in Greece.

DISTANCE: 4.5km (3-mile) walk in the Valley of the Temples; 1km (0.6 miles) walk (or car, bus or taxi) to the Museo Archeologico Regionale; (optional 3km [2 miles] from museum to modern Agrigento).

TIME: A full day

START: Valley of the Temples

END: Museo Archeologico Regionale or modern Agrigento

POINTS TO NOTE: With just one day restrict your visit of the town of Agrigento to the evening. Take a picnic to the temples and consider splashing out in the evening at Villa Athena, reserving a table overlooking the temples. For full appreciation of the ruins, an audioguide or guided tour in English is highly recommended. Ask at the entrance. Beware that in midsummer Agrigento can be unbearably hot and crowded. The Eastern Zone with the main temples is best viewed in the early morning or late afternoon – or when floodlit at night.

In its heyday, in the 5th century BC, Agrigento rivalled Athens in splendour. Known as Akragas, it comprised painted temples in a natural amphitheatre, a valley of wild thyme, silvery olive and almond groves. In the past, it was considered a sybaritic city, and Plato claimed that the people of Akragas 'built for eternity but feasted as if there were no tomorrow'.

Founded by colonists from nearby Gela and Rhodes on the south coast in 581 BC, the city prospered as a tyranny until it was sacked by the Carthaginians in 406 BC. After a Roman revival the site was destroyed by Byzantines, who razed all the 'pagan' temples except Concordia. Akragas was then abandoned until the 18th century.

Nowadays the valley remains evocative, even if the modern world intrudes with unappealing high-rise apartment blocks seen in the distance. Most of modern Agrigento is an unappetising urban mix, but it has a medieval core of intercrossing Moorish streets, well worth a visit if you have time at the end of the day.

VALLE DEI TEMPLI

The arrival point of the **Valle dei Templi** (daily Apr–June 10am–6pm, July–Sept 10am–7pm, Oct–Mar 10am–5pm; www.parcodeitempli.net; charge) is **Piazzale dei Templi** ❶, once the agora or marketplace. The archaeological park is divided into two sections: the Eastern Zone, with the main temples, and the Western Zone.

Start at the Eastern Zone (across the road), where you purchase a ticket covering both zones and follow the Via Sacra. The temples are transformed by light, and were praised by Lawrence Durrell in *Sicilian Carousel* as 'pure opalescent honey'. A local saying goes that you have not lived until you have seen the Temple of Concord change with the seasons, at dawn, dusk and moonlight. Ideally, return after dinner to see the temples glow in the black countryside, radiating security and serenity before the Mediterranean Sea.

EASTERN ZONE

Tempio di Ercole
The first treasure is the **Tempio di Ercole** ❷ (Temple of Hercules), just within the enclosure. This was designed in the Archaic Doric style in 520 BC and, as such, is the oldest temple. It once protected a statue of Hercules and had a glorious entablature emblazoned with lions, leaves and palms. Today just eight columns from the original 38 rise up from the mound of rubble. These were re-erected in 1924 by Alexander Hardcastle, a devoted Scottish archaeologist, who lived at the **Villa Aurea** ❸, a short way up on the right.

Tempio della Concordia
Follow Via Sacra to the superbly sited **Tempio della Concordia** ❹ (Temple of Concord), which, after Theseion in Athens, is the best-preserved Greek temple in the world. The tapering columns tilt inwards, creating a lofty grace that belies the weighty entablature. The temple dates from 430 BC, but was saved from destruction during the 6th century AD, when it was converted into a Christian church. The temple still represents sheer perfection in line.

Tempio di Giunone
Cool off with an iced drink or *gelato* at the café on the left as you go up. At the end of Via Sacra stands the **Tempio di Giunone** ❺ (Temple of Juno, also known as Tempio di Hera), surmounting a rocky ridge. Part of the temple fell over the hill after a landslide, but the rest is well preserved. Juno was the goddess of marriage, and her shrine is the most romantic of temples. Yet in reality it was a ghoulish spot: the stones were tinged red after the temple was licked by Carthaginian flames in 406 BC.

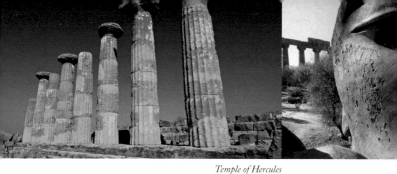

Temple of Hercules

THE WESTERN ZONE

Tempio di Giove

Return to Piazzale dei Templi and enter the Western Zone through the ticket gate. With the area of a football pitch, the **Tempio di Giove 6** (Temple of Jove, also called Zeus Olimpico) was the largest Doric temple ever known, although it was never finished. The U-shaped grooves on the stone blocks are pulley marks formed during construction. Today's rubble is indecipherable: the masonry was plundered to build the harbour walls at Porto Empedocle, the outlet for Agrigento's sulphur and potash industries. Thirty-eight telamones (colossal columns carved as male figures) were originally

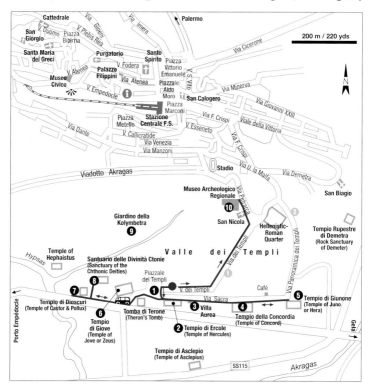

Igor Mitoraj bronze sculpture   *Temple of Hera*

built into the walls between the columns, supporting the architrave. Lying on the ground is a sandstone copy of a telamon, dreamily resting his head on his arms. As well as their aesthetic and practical functions, the telamones had allegorical significance, illustrating the war against Zeus. Like Atlas, the defeated giants were compelled to carry the world on their shoulders.

Tempio di Dioscuri

West of the Temple of Jove (Zeus Olimpico) is a puzzling quarter dotted with pagan shrines. The **Tempio di Dioscuri** ❼ (also known as Tempio di Castore e Polluce, or Castor and Pollux) was named after Zeus' twin sons. Castor was mortal and Pollux immortal, so they spent alternate days in Hades and on Mount Olympus. Graceful and evocative, the ruin is in fact an artistic pastiche, erected in 1836 from the remains of other shrines.

Just behind lies what is believed to be the 6th-century **Santuario delle Divinità Ctonie** ❽ (Sanctuary of the Chthonic Deities), concealing sacrificial altars and well-like ditches. The sanctuary is a shrine to fertility, immortality and eternal youth.

Giardino della Kolymbetra

Close to the Sanctuary, climb down to the **Giardino della Kolymbethra** ❾ (Kolymbetra Garden, May–Oct 10am–6pm, Nov–Apr 10am–5pm; separate charge, free to FAI National Trust members), a large and verdant garden of orange groves, along with almonds, olives, bananas and numerous other Mediterranean trees and plants. The Greek garden began life as a vast pool, used originally for sacred rites and later for agriculture. It has been restored and provides a delightful diversion from the Temples and a perfect spot for a picnic, sitting on a bench under orange trees.

MUSEO ARCHEOLOGICO

A short drive or 1km (0.6-mile) walk up Via dei Templi from Piazzale dei Templi leads past **Villa Athena**, with sublime views from the restaurant, see ❶, to the Archaeological Museum, the Hellenistic-Roman quarter and a clutch of pagan shrines. The fortifications which you can see en route are a reminder that Agrigento was once enclosed by walls, towers and massive gates.

The **Museo Archeologico Regionale** ❿ (Regional Archaeological Museum; Tue–Sun 9am–7.30pm, Mon 9am–1.30pm; charge, combined ticket with temples) incorporates a church, courtyard and temple foundations, and a wealth of artefacts found during excavations at the Valley of the Temples. This is an excellent museum, with labels in English – you could easily spend half a day here. Highlights are the black and red Attic vases, the section on the Temple of Jove (or Zeus Olimpico) in Room 6, including temple reconstructions and a 7.65m (25ft) tall reconstructed telemon, the marble *ephebe* (classical

View of Agrigento from the Temple of Jove

youth) in Room 10 and the child's sarcophogus in Room 11.

If you're calling it a day you might consider an early seafood dinner at **Trattoria dei Templi**, see , 300m/yds east of the museum.

MODERN AGRIGENTO

Crowning the ridge to the north of the Valley of Temples, modern Agrigento occupies the site of the Greek Acropolis. Most visitors skip the city, deterred by the outlying sprawl, distance on foot from the temples or parking problems. (There are buses from the Valle dei Templi, or it's a quick ride in a taxi.)

The old part of town has a tatty medieval charm, though restoration has begun, very slowly, on a handful of historic buildings. The main **Via Atenea** is a pleasant street for strolling with smart shops and plenty of restaurants.

The most notable monument is the church of **Santo Spirito** (erratic openings, ring for the custodian at No. 11 Salita S. Spirito; donation expected). This is the church of a late 13th-century Cistercian convent whose nuns specialise in making and selling sweet almond and pistachio pastries. Ring the door bell marked '*monastero*' and say '*Vorrei dei dolci*' (I would like some pastries), and have plenty of euros ready (these are not charity cakes). The church is rather dilapidated but inside has fine Baroque stuccowork attributed to Giacomo Serpotta. To the northwest **Santa Maria dei Greci**

(8am–noon, 3.30–6.30pm) is a Norman church set among Agrigento's alleyways in the heart of the medieval quarter. Below ground is the greatest surprise: the church is constructed around a 5th-century Greek temple.

The **Cattedrale** (daily 9am–12.30pm, 4–6.30pm) on top of the hill incorporates Arab-Norman, Catalan Gothic and Baroque elements. The Norman Gothic nave boasts an inlaid, coffered ceiling, while the graceful Baroque stuccowork in the choir contrasts with a severe Gothic chapel.

Food and Drink

① VILLA ATHENA
Via Passeggiata Archeologica 33; tel: 0922 596 288; L and D daily; www.athena hotels.it; €€€€.
This lovely five-star villa-hotel with restaurant scores highly on atmosphere and for magical views across the Valley of the Temples. This is the place for a romantic dinner on the terrace, based on seafood or herb-flavoured roast meats. Reservations advisable.

② TRATTORIA DEI TEMPLI
Via Panoramica dei Templi 15; tel: 0922 403 110; L and D Mon–Sat; €€
Fish and seafood dominate the menu at this vaulted, rustic retreat near the temples. Fish of the day is always a good bet. Reservations advisable.

Highly perched Enna

ENNA AND VILLA ROMANA

*Explore the dramatically sited mountain city of Enna, then visit **Piazza Armerina** and Sicily's great Villa Romana, with the finest in-situ **Roman floor mosaics in existence**.*

DISTANCE: 68km (42 miles)
TIME: A full day
START: Enna
END: Villa Romana
POINTS TO NOTE: Restoration of the Villa Romana has been ongoing for 10 years, so some rooms may be off limits (check www.villaromanadelcasale.org for details; Italian only).

Enna is the highest city in Sicily, lying 900m (3,000ft) above vast plains which once supplied the Greeks and Romans with wheat. This former stronghold is an introspective city, often shrouded in mist – yet a welcome relief after the silent landscape that surrounds it. On the way to Villa Romana, stop briefly at the hill town of Piazza Armerina. Some of the town's late medieval palazzi and churches are crumbling but restoration is ongoing.

ENNA

Enna ❶ is 85km (52 miles) west of Catania on autostrada A19, or 88km (55 miles) northeast of Agrigento on the winding SS640.

On a clear day there are fabulous views from Enna, and the best place to enjoy them is from the tallest tower, **Torre Pisano**, one of six surviving Norman and Swabian towers of the **Castello di Lombardia** (daily 9am–4pm Nov–Mar, 9am–8pm Apr–Aug, 9am–6pm Sep–Oct; free). You can park near the castle, then after your visit make your way down to **Via Roma**, the main street, which is flanked by dignified mansions and churches. The **Duomo** (Cathedral; daily 9am–1pm and 3.30–8pm; free) was begun by Eleanor of Aragon in 1307 but rebuilt in a mixture of Gothic and Baroque styles. Enna's second medieval fortification is the isolated **Torre di Federico**, a tumbledown Swabian tower, on top of a hill towards Enna Bassa, the lower town.

After lunch in Enna, either at **Centrale**, see ❶, or **Ariston**, see ❷, take the SS561 from Enna Bassa, then join the SS117 bis. The steep switchback road takes you via isolated farms, rough pastures and undulating wheatfields.

The town of Aidone

AIDONE

Shortly before Piazza Armerina, turn left onto the SS288, signed **Aidone ❷**. At the top of the old town is the **Museo Archeologico** (Tue–Sun 9am–6.30pm; charge, includes site of Morgantina). Pride of place goes to the magnificent Greek statue **Venere di Morgantina**, a life-size Venus which was looted by tomb-robbers in the 1950s from the nearby Greek settlement of Morgantina. The statue mysteriously found its way to the Getty Museum in the States. After much wrangling, it was returned to Sicily in 2010, fully restored.

The site of **Morgantina ❸** (4km/2.5 miles northeast of Aidone; daily 9am–1 hour before sunset; charge, see above) lies in lovely quiet countryside with Greek remains spreading over two hills.

PIAZZA ARMERINA

The region's most inviting restaurant, **Al Fogher**, see ❽, has an unlikely setting just after the SS117/SS288 junction 3km (2 miles) before **Piazza Armerina ❹**. On arrival in the town, take the stairways and alleys up to the green-domed Baroque **Cattedrale** (8.30am–noon, 4.30–6pm) which crowns one hill and dominates the town. The church has a venerated icon, the Madonna delle Vittorie, seen only during the Palio dei Normanni, which in August re-enacts the taking of the town from the Saracens by Norman Count Roger in 1087. On the same square the sober 18th-century **Palazzo Trigona** is being turned into the city museum. Via Floresta beside the palace leads down to the dilapidated Aragonese **Castello** (no access). Cobbled **Via Monte**, leading off Piazza del Duomo, was the main street in medieval times and still retains some of its former palazzi.

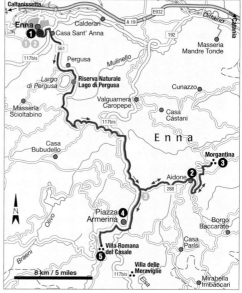

Aidone museum artefacts

The famous 'Bikini Girls' mosaic

VILLA ROMANA

From Piazza Armerina follow signs to **Villa Romana del Casale ➎** (daily 9am–6pm; charge) nestling among thick woodland 5.5km (3.5 miles) away. Co-emperor Maximian, who ruled the waning Roman Empire with Diocletian, is said to have built this magnificent villa. It was later occupied by the Norman kings before disappearing under a landslide for 700 years. Excavations began in 1950 when a hoard of treasure was discovered.

Mosaics

The exquisite Roman-African mosaics are the villa's key attraction. All the scenes normally excluded from Christian art lie in this kaleidoscope of life, celebrating hunting and fishing, dancing and discus-throwing, massage and lovemaking.

The entrance is via the *thermae* (baths). The centrepiece is the **Courtyard**, with a peristyle, pool and mosaic pairings of domestic and wild animals. The **Salone del Circo** (Circus Hall) has a vibrant depiction of a frenetic chariot race at the Circus Maximus in Rome. Off the courtyard, the **Room of the Cupid Fishermen** depicts a dolphin-riding mermaid. Edging the main courtyard is the 60m/yd long **Corridor of the Great Hunt**, with mosaics of a sea separating Africa and Europe, and a swirling mass of movement with chariots, lions, cheetahs and rhinos. The **Room of Ten Maidens** presents the Villa's most famous mosaic of 'the Bikini Girls', with

10 scantily clad girl gymnasts. The **Triclinium** (Great Hall) is the villa's masterpiece, with the central mosaic showing the Twelve Labours of Hercules.

The perspex covering the rooms has caused a hothouse effect which deteriorated the mosaics. The ongoing restoration includes roofing that reflects the original Roman design.

For dinner, best to go back to Al Fogher.

Food and Drink

① CENTRALE

Piazza VI Dicembre 9, Enna; tel: 0935 500 963; L and D Sun–Fri, D Sat; €€
This long-established restaurant serves good, reasonably priced family fare. Benito Mussolini's signature is in the guestbook.

② ARISTON

Via Roma 353, Enna; tel: 0935 26038; L and D daily; €€
This popular eatery has hearty portions of traditional Sicilian fish and meat dishes. Good pizzas too (evenings only).

③ AL FOGHER

Contrada Bellia, Piazza Armerina; tel: 0935 684123; L and D Tue–Sat, L Sun; www.alfogher.net; €€–€€€
Chef Angelo produces artful creations made with the freshest of ingredients. Specialities include crispy fillet of red mullet. Save space for the chocolate pyramid dessert. Reservations advisable.

Siracusa harbour

SIRACUSA

Alluring Siracusa is the summation of Sicilian splendour. The twin poles of attraction are the Greek archaeological park of Neapolis and seductive Ortigia, the island that is the city's cultural heart.

DISTANCE: 6km (3.75 miles) on foot; or 4km (2.5 miles) on foot and 2km (1.25 miles) by car, bus or taxi
TIME: A full day
START: Parco Archeologico della Neapolis
END: Ortigia
POINTS TO NOTE: The Parco Archeologico della Neapolis, where you can park, is 2km (1.25 miles) from the historic centre of Ortigia. Frequent buses link the two. Parking in central Ortigia is limited to residents, so use the cheap multi-storey Parcheggio Talete, Via Veneto, and take the shuttle bus or walk to the centre.

Siracusa was one of the great powers of the ancient world, eventually surpassing Athens in prestige. The decisive battle was Siracusa's defeat of Athens at sea in 413 BC. Under Dionysius the Elder, the tyrant and monumental builder, the city had the grandest public works in the Western world. Archimedes, who was born here, was among its citizens. The Roman siege of Siracusa (213–211 BC) was marked by his ingenuity in devising mechanical devices to foil the enemy, including mirrors and magnifying lenses to blind them and perhaps even burn their boats. The Romans finally subdued the city in 211 BC, and in the 9th century it was destroyed by Arabs. As an early Christian centre, Siracusa was evangelised by St Peter and St Paul, and extensive catacombs served as both tombs and churches.

After decades of neglect, the island of Ortigia has undergone regeneration and is looking lovelier than ever.

PARCO ARCHEOLOGICO DELLA NEAPOLIS

Northwest of the centre, the **Parco Archeologico della Neapolis** (Archaeological Park of Neapolis; Via Augusto [well signed]; daily 9am–2 hours before sunset; charge) is the city's famed Classical park, set among firs and olives. It contains rough-hewn quarries, tombs and caverns, but the focus is the vast and grandiose Greek Theatre.

Teatro Greco

Passing the rubble of **Ara di Ierone II** ❶, a huge sacrificial altar once decorated by telamones (stone giants), you get to the **Teatro Greco** ❷ (Greek Theatre). The open theatre, seating 15,000, is one of the largest and best-preserved in existence. It dates from 474 BC, though it was altered and added to by the Romans. Under the Greeks the theatre witnessed works by Sophocles, Euripides and Aeschylus, but during the Roman era it became an amphitheatre for gladiatorial combat. The theatre tradition is maintained today with Classical Greek dramas staged (in Italian) daily from the second week of May to the end of June (www.indafondazione.org).

Latomie

From the theatre a path leads down to the *latomie*, giant quarries which were used for the building of the ancient city, and more famously, as open-air prisons during the war with Athens (413 BC).

The **Orecchio di Dionisio** ❸ (Ear of Dionysius), a 47m (154ft) high arched cavern with remarkable acoustics, attracts almost as much tourist attention as the Greek Theatre. Carved into the rock and shaped like an upside-down ear lobe, it was supposedly employed by Dionysius to eavesdrop on his captives.

Beyond the cavern are the lemon-scented quarries which were once used as a prison.

The adjoining **Grotta dei Cordari** (Ropemakers' Cave; closed indefinitely) is scored with chisel marks, because it was here that ropemakers stretched out their damp strands and tested their ropes for stress.

The largest of the quarries is the **Latomia del Paradiso** ❹, now a lush and colourful garden abounding in rocky arches, cacti, olive trees and citrus groves.

A separate entrance leads to the **Anfiteatro Romano** ❺ (Roman Amphitheatre), ringed by trees. Built in the 3rd century AD, it staged circuses and gladiatorial events. Exiting the park, take Via Augusto, then cross over the main road for Viale Teocrito.

BASILICA AND CATACOMBS OF SAN GIOVANNI

Other remnants of ancient Siracusa are scattered about the city. A much-visited site is the **Basilica of San Giovanni** ❻, signed to the left off Viale Teocrito. Formerly the cathedral of Siracusa, this is now a rather charming roofless ruin in a wild garden, but looks incongruous in its modern surrounds. Crooked steps lead down to the crypt of St Marcian, who was flogged to death in AD 254.

The **catacombe di San Giovanni** (San Giovanni Catacombs; daily 9.30am–12.30pm, 2.30–5.30pm, until 4.30pm in winter; charge, guided tours only) are an eerie network of catacombs, with thousands of empty niches (looted by grave robbers) used until the 6th century. Fragments of frescoes and arcane symbols etched in the stone are still visible.

Orecchio di Dionisio

Museo Archeologico

Opposite the ugly modern **Madonna delle Lácrime**, built to house a statue of the Madonna which reputedly wept for five days in 1953, the recently restored **Museo Archeologico Paolo Orsi** ❼ (Villa Landolina; charge) is Sicily's largest archaeological collection and one of

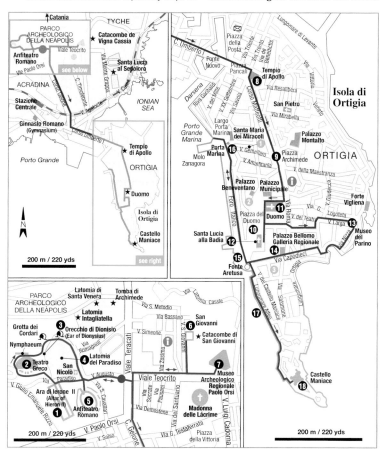

Museo Archeologico jars   *Excursion boat*

the most important in Italy. It is divided into four sections: prehistory (A), Greek colonies in Sicily (B), sub-colonies and Hellenised centres (C) and Greek and Roman Siracusa (D). This is a huge and very confusing museum, with 18,000 pieces and long complex explanations (some in Italian only). To take it all in you would need several hours; alternatively, concentrate on the treasure trove of Classical statuary found in Siracusa. The prize piece is the headless and voluptuous **Venere Anadiomene** (Section D), also known as Venus Landolina because it was unearthed in the grounds of the Villa Landolina which houses the museum. There is also an Archaic fertility goddess suckling twins and a voracious Medusa with her tongue lolling out.

ORTIGIA

Avoid the dreary walk to Ortigia by taking a bus (No. 1, 3 or 12 from Viale Teracati near the Archaeological Park, tickets from *tabacchi*) or a taxi (rank opposite the Archaeological Park); otherwise drive to the Talete car park at Ortigia. Start your walk through this atmospheric and picturesque island at the ruins of the **Tempio di Apollo ❽** (565 BC), dedicated to the huntress Artemis (Diana) and her brother. If you are up for some local produce, stop first at Ortigia's lively market (Mon–Sat 8am–2pm), just steps away from the Tempio. This is also where most of Siracusa's most atmospheric restaurants are. Specialities include sea-

food, especially swordfish and shrimps, stuffed artichokes and *stimpirata di coniglio*, a rabbit and vegetable dish.

THE CENTRE

From the temple it is a short stroll up the shopping street, Corso Matteotti, to **Piazza Archimede ❾**. This grand Baroque stage set is framed by dignified mansions and focuses on a circular fountain of the river nymph Arethusa being transformed into a spring. For good restaurants head for Via Gemmellaro, via the narrow Via Scinia off the main square. **Archimede**, see ❶, serves excellent seafood and antipasti.

Piazza del Duomo
From Piazza Archimede, stroll south along the main **Via Roma**, then right for **Piazza del Duomo ❿**. The terrace of the **Grand Caffè del Duomo**, see ❷, affords fine views. This is one of the most beautiful squares in Sicily, irregular in shape and flanked by a harmonious variety of Baroque buildings. Built over a temple to Athena, the **Duomo ⓫** (Cathedral; daily 7.30am–7.30pm; free) is a summation of Sicilian history, with Byzantine apses, a Norman font, a medieval ceiling and Baroque facade and choir. Classical columns bulge through the external walls in Via Minerva, proof that the 5th-century BC temple was converted into a church in the 7th century AD. Cicero left a famous description of the sumptuous

Fonte Aretusa at night

original decoration of the temple: walls painted with battle scenes and heroic portraits, doors of gold and ivory and a huge statue of the goddess Athena on the roof carrying a golden shield which flashed in the sun like a beacon for distant ships. Now the interior of the cathedral is impressively bare; the beamed roof, rough piers and patterned marble floor all reinforce the impression of a living Greek temple.

Among the fine palaces overlooking the piazza are the **Palazzo Municipale** (1629), the city council, north of the Duomo, and opposite the elegant **Palazzo Beneventano**, with a beautiful courtyard, which housed Nelson in 1789. South of the Duomo is the Pala-

zzo Arcivescovile (Archbishop's Palace), with overhanging lemon trees and the late 17th-century church of **Santa Lucia alla Badia** ⑫ (Tue−Sun 11am−4pm), now home to Caravaggio's masterpiece the *Burial of St Lucy* (1608).

Papyrus Museum

Walk back towards the Piazza and turn left, then follow the signs to the **Museo del Papiro** ⑬ (Papyrus Museum; Via Nizza 14; Tue−Sun 9am−1pm; free; www.museodelpapiro.it). The collection is now housed in a renovated convent and displays ancient papyrus manuscripts, Egyptian papyruses, along with papyrus boats, sandals and rope, and an interesting selection of writing utensils from various eras. Siracusa is the only place in Europe where papyrus grows wild. You can see it on the banks of the Ciane River near Siracusa, also in the Fonte Aretusa in Ortigia (see below).

South of Piazza del Duomo

Beyond the piazza go down Via Picherali, then cross Piazza San Rocco and turn right for Via Capodieci. If staying for dinner, book a table at **Da Mariano**, see ❸, on Vicolo Zuccolà just off Via Capodieci. Further on, **Palazzo Bellomo** is the loveliest Catalan Gothic mansion in Ortigia, and home to the **Galleria Regionale** ⑭ (Tue−Sat 9am−7pm, Sun 9am−1pm; charge). This is a collection of Sicilian 17th- and 18th-century paintings, the star of which is Antonello da Messina's *Annunciazione*.

Boat cruises

If you need a break from walking, try a boat trip from Porto Grande: a short trip around Ortigia passes the Swabian fortress of Castello Maniace, offering windswept views of the rocky Lungomare d'Ortigia. A more adventurous cruise is along the Fiume Ciane, a river 7km (4 miles) southwest of Siracusa off the SS115. The boat passes through groves of papyrus with cobweb-like tendrils and takes in the remains of the 6th-century Tempio di Giove Olimpico. For information on boat trips, visit www.compagniadel selene.it, or Via Malta 63. Boat cruises only operate in season, normally from April to September.

Diving in Ortigia   *Thirteen-century Castello Maniace*

THE WATERFRONT

Follow Via Capodieci to the seafront and the **Fonte Aretusa** ⓯, a freshwater spring venerated throughout the ancient world. Legend has it that the nymph Arethusa was fleeing the unwanted attentions of the river god Alpheius. As the nymph reached Ortigia, the Olympian goddess Artemis (Diana) transformed her into a fountain, only for Alpheius to pull her under the waves and 'mingle his waters with hers'.

Originally a valuable source of water for the island, it was thought to be a resurgence of a river that disappeared underground at Olympia.

The tree-lined **Foro Italico** promenade runs north to **Porta Marina** ⓰, a gateway created in the 15th century as part of the Spanish fortifications, and beyond it **Porto Grande Marina**, where you could cool off with a fresh fruit drink or watermelon *granita* while watching excursion and fishing boats come and go.

The promenade running south from Fonte Aretusa is the **Lungomare Alfeo** ⓱, where you can join the evening *passeggiata* or enjoy the sunset and sea views over an *aperitivo* in one of the bars. Marking the end of the peninsula is **Castello Maniace** ⓲ (Tue–Sun 10am–1pm; charge), built by Frederick II in 1239. This massive Swabian fortress has been newly restored and opened to the public. The sea views alone are worth a visit.

Food and Drink

① ARCHIMEDE
Via Gemellaro 8, Ortigia; tel: 0931 69701; www.trattoriaarchimede.it; L and D Mon–Sat, also Sun Dec–Feb; €€
Something of an institution in Ortigia, Archimede has been going since 1938. Expect friendly service and a wide range of seafood pastas, half a dozen couscous dishes and a couple of meat options. Pizzas are also available, and there is a verandah.

② GRAN CAFFÈ DEL DUOMO
Piazza del Duomo 18, Ortigia; Tue–Sun 7am–7pm; €
The service isn't always friendly and the pastries are average, but you can't beat this café for views of the Duomo and the square. If you crave something sweet and Sicilian, try their *cannoli* (pastry tube filled with sweet ricotta) or cool off with a gelato.

③ DA MARIANO
Vicolo Zuccolà 9, Ortigia; tel: 0931 67444; www.osteriadamariano.it; L and D Wed–Mon; €
This is an authentic *osteria* with a welcoming atmosphere. The emphasis is on food from the Iblei mountains: antipasti of ricotta and pistachio nuts, *salumi*, olives, marinated vegetables, followed by rustic pastas and meat dishes.

Church of San Domenico, Noto

THE VAL DI NOTO

Sicily's corner of Baroque splendour, currently the most dynamic region of the island, ideally calls for a couple of days' exploration. This tour takes in the finest of the towns: Noto, Módica, Scicli, Ragusa, and includes a picnic in the lush gorge of Cava d'Íspica.

DISTANCE: 110km (68 miles) from Siracusa
TIME: 2 days
START: Noto
END: Ragusa
POINTS TO NOTE: Módica makes a good base: it has some lovely hotels, B&Bs and restaurants. Alternatively consider Scicli or Ragusa.

The Val di Noto is currently the most dynamic part of Sicily. The Unesco-listed Baroque cities, built after the terrible earthquake of 1693, were designed to be theatrical and spectacular and are now being restored to their former glory. The churches and palaces are particularly fine seen after dark when the honey-coloured stone is lit up to magical effect.

If coming from Siracusa, take the A18, exit Noto, and head for the centre.

NOTO

After the old **Noto Antica** was razed in the 1693 earthquake, Prince Landolina and Giuseppe Lanza (Duke of Camastra) lost no time in creating the new Noto on the flanks of a distant hill. Today it is the finest Baroque town in Sicily, with magnificently restored churches and palaces. On the lower slopes, three scenic squares unfold in a succession of dramatic perspectives, sculpted in golden stone.

Corso Vittorio Emanuele and Piazza Municipio

Arriving in the centre of **Noto ❶**, park alongside the **Giardini Pubblici** (Public Gardens) or behind the stadium and enter through the monumental **Porta Reale** gateway for the **Corso Vittorio Emanuele**. Conveniently, all of Noto's finest buildings are on or just off this pedestrianised main thoroughfare. On the right, at the top of a theatrical, grand flight of stairs, stands the church of **San Francesco** (daily 9.30am–12.30pm, 4–7pm; free). Alongside it sits the old monastery of **San Salvatore**, and on the same piazza the richly decorated church of **Santa Chiara** (daily 9.30am–1pm, 3.30–8pm in summer, 10am–noon in winter; charge for tower). It's worth climb-

Palazzo Nicolaci's interior	*Palazzo Nicolaci's ornate balconies*

ing the tower, up a steep spiral staircase, for the fabulous views at the top.

The Corso sweeps on to the majestic **Piazza Municipio**, on which stands the elegantly grand **Palazzo Ducezio** (Town Hall, with the Hall of Mirrors; daily 9.30am–6pm; charge), and facing it the splendid **Cattedrale di San Niccolò** (entrance on Via Cavour; daily 9am–1pm, 4–7pm; charge). In 1996 the cupola and roof of the cathedral collapsed, but the building has since been restored to its former glory.

Palazzo Villadorata

Stop for coffee and pastries at **Caffè Sicilia**, see 1, across the road at No.

125, then take Via Corrado Nicolaci, almost opposite, where you will find the grandest mansion in town: the restored **Palazzo Nicolaci di Villadorata** (daily 10am–noon, 3–5.30pm; charge). This Baroque jewel has wonderful balconies decorated with friezes of griffins, mythical monsters, horses and cherubs. The interior is equally grand, with frescoed walls and ceilings. Opposite the palace, call in for a glass of wine or light lunch at **Cantina Modica di San Giovanni**, see 1, and see the private museum of Alessandro Modica while sampling delicacies from this young baron's wine estate.

Back on the Corso, continue on to **Piazza XVI Maggio**, graced by gardens of

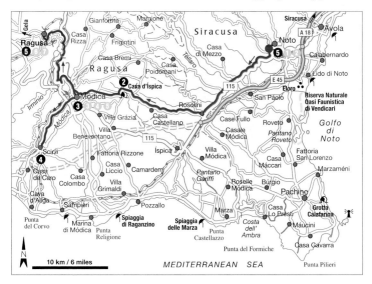

Cherubs on the church of Santa Chiara

palms, monkey puzzle trees and a fountain of Hercules. Dominating is Gagliardi's masterpiece, the church of **San Domenico**, and facing it, the tiny and ornate **Teatro Comunale** (1850) (daily 9.30am–1.30pm, 3–7pm; charge). Concerts are held here from October to May.

CAVA D'ÍSPICA

From Noto take the SS 115 south, signed Ragusa and Rosolino. Just after Rosolino, take the inconspicuous turning on the right just after the Agip petrol station. Then follow signs for the **Cava d'Íspica ❷** (Tue–Sat 9am–1pm; charge), a 13km (8-mile) long limestone gorge which, with its catacombs and cave dwellings, makes a fascinating walk – even if you only do a short section. Just below the entrance is the **Catacomba Larderia**, early Christian catacombs, while close to the car park, the **Grotta di San Nicola** is a rock chapel with badly damaged late Byzantine frescoes, that was inhabited until the 1950s.

MÓDICA

Perched on a ridge spilling down into a gorge, **Módica ❸** is two towns in one: **Módica Alta** (high) and **Módica Bassa** (low). At first sight the setting is more prepossessing than the grey–brown town, but Módica repays exploration, from its mysterious alleys and mouth-watering food to its illutrious history as the most powerful fiefdom on the island. Although it is the most prosperous town, in Sicily it is an unpretentious sort of place, far from glitzy, even shabby in parts. On Easter Day, Sicilians don their Sunday best and flock to Módica for the festival of the Madonna Vasa Vasa. A statue of the Madonna in mourning, seeking her son, is paraded through the streets. When she meets the resurrected Christ her mantle changes from black to blue, doves fly out, bells peal and a jubilant crowd applauds the embrace (*vasa vasa*) of mother and son. This is one of the most moving and famous religious festivals in Sicily. Módica is also famous for its chocolate, which is sweet and slightly gritty.

Corso Umberto I

Follow signs to the centre and, once through the sprawling outskirts, you will arrive at **Corso Umberto** in Módica Bassa where you can usually find a parking space (tickets from *tabacchi*). This is the town's main street and it is flanked by the golden facades of palaces and churches, along with smart boutiques, wine bars and gourmet delights. A theatrical flight of steps, flanked by life-size statues of the 12 apostles, leads up to the opulent **Cattedrale di San Pietro** (daily 9am–1pm, 4–7.30pm; free). Nearby, off Via Grimaldi, is the inconspicuous entrance to the ancient **San Niccolò Inferiore** (ring the bell for entry; charge), a grotto-like church, where three layers of frescoes dating from the 11th century were discovered in 1989.

San Pietro painting, Módica   *View of Módica*

Módica Alta

The pride of Módica is the **Duomo di San Giorgio** (Cathedral of St George; 9am–1pm, 4–7pm), perched precariously above the alleys of historic Módica Alta and ideally approached by the 250-step staircase (you can also access it by road). A masterpiece by Gagliardi, the church boasts a sumptuous three-tiered Baroque facade and a soaring belfry, silhouetted against the sky. There are good views of Módica's rooftops from the terrace, but even better ones if you go higher to **San Giovanni Evangelista**, another grandiose Baroque church with a monumental flight of steps. At the end of Via Pizzo nearby, a belvedere known as **Il Pizzo** affords fine views over the town. After exploration of the upper town, consider dining at the gastronomic **La Gazza Ladra**, see ❸, or the cheaper **Locanda del Colonnello**, see ❹, both part of the charming Palazzo Failla hotel.

Alternatively join the locals in the *passeggiata* (evening stroll) along Corso Umberto I below, then dine at **Fattoria delle Torri**, see ❺, which is tucked away in an alley across the Corso from Piazza Matteoti.

SCICLI

One of the smallest of the eight World Heritage towns, **Scicli** ❹ is a Baroque gem, lying in a valley surrounded by rocky hills. Take the scenic SP54 southwest from Módica (10km/6.25 miles) to reach Scicli, which until recently was little visited. But this 'theatre of stone' is seeing a new lease of life – palazzi and churches have been skilfully restored, artisans are moving in, and the town has come into its own as a film set (see box).

The town lacks the symmetry of Noto but has some fine church facades and bizarrely adorned palaces. The best-preserved Baroque street is **Via F. M. Penna**, overlooked by the elegant church of **San Giovanni**. Of the town palaces the most remarkable is **Palazzo Beneventano**, whose balconies are embellished with fantastic corbels representing mythical beasts, Moors and ghoulish human masks.

From here you can follow the signs up the hill that dominates the town, along an attractive winding path that leads to the ruins of medieval fortifications. Near the top you will reach the restored remains of the church of **San Matteo**. This was part of a medieval settlement, and cave-homes here, which were inhabited until the 1980s, now serve as wine cellars, garages and storerooms.

RAGUSA

Return towards Módica along the SP54, then follow the SS115 to **Ragusa** ❺ (25.5km/16 miles). When Ragusa was reduced to rubble by the 1693 earthquake, the merchants built bland

Church of San Giovanni in Scicli

Ragusa Alta on the hill, but the aristocracy recreated **Ragusa Ibla** on the original valley site. The two merged as one town in 1926.

Ragusa Ibla

Ignore Ragusa Alta and follow the gorge crossed by three bridges to the Baroque city of Ragusa Ibla. Follow signs and leave the car in the large car park below **Piazza della Repubblica**. From here it is a 10-minute walk down to the centre of Ragusa Ibla. But first admire the stunning views of Ibla from **Santa Maria delle Scale** to the south-west. From this balcony over the town, the energetic can take the winding 250 steps down.

Ibla is an enchanting, timeless pocket of Sicily, where old-world charm and intimacy prevail. Gentrification has reversed the neglect in recent years; crumbling mansions are being restored, historic palaces have been converted to restaurants, bars and gourmet delis, and where once Ibla was deserted after dark, its pedestrianised quarter is now the focus for Ragusa's low-key nightlife.

Gagliardi's blue-domed **Cattedrale di San Giorgio** (daily 7am–12.30pm, 3–7pm) is set high above **Piazza del Duomo**, the palm-lined cobbled piazza. The terraced cathedral is a masterpiece of graceful, swelling rhythms, embellished with decorative swirls and frills. Follow a visit to the cathedral with a stroll around the atmospheric Jewish ghetto, behind the church. Then if it's time for sustenance, head either to **Il Duomo**, see ❶, for a gastronomic blow-out, or try the good-value **Il Barocco**, see ❼, on Via Orfanotrofio to the east.

The main **Corso XXV Aprile**, on a hill, is lined by a selection of inviting eateries, food shops and galleries. Across the square at the end of the street, take a moment of reflection in the **Giardino Ibleo**, an exotic park with ruined churches, victims of the 1693 earthquake. This is a popular spot for an evening stroll, with great views.

The Montalbano trail

On your travels through Ragusa province you are more than likely to see references to Montalbano, the detective in the popular TV series adapted from the detective novels by Antonio Camilleri and filmed in the region. The novels have become the best-read books to come out of Italy since *The Leopard*. Montalbano aficionados can follow the detective's footsteps and sit in his office in Scicli's Comune (Town Hall), which doubles as his office in the fictional town of Vigata. Scicli's churches and convoluted Baroque facades feature in most episodes of the series. So popular are the books and TV series in Italy there are Montalbano-themed holiday packages, as well as bus tours and train trips.

View of Ragusa

Driving through Ragusa Ibla

Food and Drink

① CAFFÈ SICILIA

Corso Vittorio Emanuele 125, Noto; Tue–
Sun 8am–10pm, closed Feb and two weeks
in Mar; €

This is one of Sicily's most celebrated
pasticcerie, dating from 1892, with home-
made pastries, almond cakes, *granite*,
cassata and ice creams.

② CANTINA MODICA DI SAN GIOVANNI

Palazzo Modica, Via Nicolaci, Noto; tel: 345
369 3045; 10am–midnight daily; €–€€

Alessandro Modica owns this ancestral
palazzo. His delightful wine bar and inn
serves award-winning wines from the family
estate matched by unfussy dishes, including
cheeses and salami from the Monti Iblei and
fish from the *tonnara* in Marzamemi.

③ LA GAZZA LADRA

Via Blandini 5, Módica Alta; tel: 0932 755
655; www.ristorantelagazzaladra.it; L and D
Tue–Sat and L and D Sun; €€€

This Michelin-starred restaurant is run
by renowned chef David Tamburini in the
boutique hotel Palazzo Failla. The ambience
is ultra refined, while the cuisine has Sicilian
roots, with a nouvelle twist.

④ LA LOCANDA DEL COLONNELLO

Vico Biscari 6, Piazza S. Teresa, Módica Alta;
tel: 0932 752 423; L & D Thur–Tue; €€

La Gazza Ladra's chef has opened an inn
celebrating 'cucina povera', rustic cuisine
inspired by the simplest produce. Dishes
feature *i ceci* (chickpeas), green fava beans
and *il sugo* (tomato sauce). Try the creamy
broad bean soup with roasted octopus and
wild fennel.

⑤ FATTORIA DELLE TORRI

Vico Napolitano 14, Módica Alta; tel: 0932
751 286; L & D Tue–Sat, L Sun; €€–€€€

This charming *trattoria* serves wonderful
traditional fare in a Baroque palatial setting.
Dinner is served under lemon trees in warm
weather. Reservations are essential.

⑥ IL DUOMO

Via Capitano Boccheri 31, Ragusa Ibla; tel:
0932 651 265; www.ristoranteduomo.it; L
and D Tue–Sat, D Mon; €€€–€€€€

Arguably the best restaurant in Sicily, the
elegant Duomo is renowned for intense,
elaborate reinterpretations of Sicilian
cuisine, as Baroque as Ibla itself. Celebrated
chef Ciccio Sultano wins awards for his
inventive cooking.

⑦ IL BAROCCO

Via Orfanotrofio 29, Ragusa Ibla; tel: 0932
652 397; L and D Thur–Tue; closed 2 weeks
Aug; www.ilbarocco.it; €–€€

Within a palazzo, this popular restaurant/
pizzeria offers good house antipasti and
a wide range of pastas. The wine list
demonstrates the oenophilic strides Sicily
has made in recent years. There are 130
labels, all from the island. Barocco also has
an *enoteca* (wine bar) just down the road.

The cathedral

CATANIA

Brave the industrial sprawl of Sicily's commercial powerhouse and discover a vibrant centre of bold Baroque buildings, boisterous food markets and cutting-edge arts and entertainment. Major restoration is ongoing, putting what was formerly a dilapidated and undervalued city on the tourist map.

DISTANCE: 4km (2.5 miles)
TIME: A half-day walk
START: Castello Ursino
END: Villa Bellini
POINTS TO NOTE: The market and some sites are closed on Sunday.

Catania lies in the shadow of brooding Mount Etna. In 1669 it unleashed a great torrent of lava that flowed over the city walls. Reconstruction was under way when the great earthquakes of 1693 swallowed up the city. Giovanni Battista Vaccarini, a Palermitan architect influenced by grand Roman Baroque, rebuilt the entire city, using the sombre black lava stone.

Castello Ursino

Start at Piazza Federico II di Svevia, dominated by the 13th-century **Castello Ursino ❶**, former fortress of Frederick II and a rare surviving pre-earthquake vestige. The fortress overlooked the Ionian Sea before Etna's lava flow pushed the coastline a quarter of a mile sea-wards. It now houses the **Museo Civico** (Civic Museum; Mon–Sat 7am–1pm, 2.30–7pm, Sun 9am–1.30pm).

Head north from the piazza, turn right into Via Transito and follow your nose (literally) for the Fish Market.

Fish Market

At the raucous **Pescheria ❷** (Fish Market; Mon–Sat 7am–2pm), sea bream, swordfish, sea urchins, squirming eels and lobsters are laid out together with meat carcasses, sheep's heads, fruit, veg and herbs. **Osteria Antica Marina**, see ❶, is renowned for fish (book ahead).

Food and Drink

❶ OSTERIA ANTICA MARINA

Via Pardo 29; tel: 095 348 197;
www.anticamarina.it; L and D Thur–Tue;
€€€
This osteria is in the heart of the Fish Market, so the fish couldn't be fresher. Choose from fish antipasti, pasta dishes with seafood sauces, and grilled fish.

Fontana dell'Elefante statue   *Catania fish market*

Piazza del Duomo

Take the steps up by the fountains to **Piazza del Duomo ❸**, the Baroque centrepiece of the city. In the centre Vaccarini's delightful **Fontana dell'Elefante** is the city symbol. Rebuilt after the earthquake, the Baroque **Duomo** (Cathedral; daily 7am–noon, 2–7pm, Sun 7.30am–noon and 4.30–7pm; free) houses the tombs of Aragonese royals and of the composer Bellini.

Via Vittorio Emanuele II

On Piazza San Francesco, the **Museo Belliniano ❹** (Mon–Sat 9am–7pm and Sun 9am–1pm; charge) was the birth-place of the composer Bellini in 1801 and houses his death mask and opera scores. The **Teatro Romano ❺** (daily 9am–1pm and 2.30–5pm; charge) was the venue for battles between exotic beasts and gladiators.

Via Crociferi and San Nicolò

From Piazza San Francesco go north along **Via Crociferi** lined with lofty 18th-century Baroque churches, convents and palazzi. Turn left at Via Gesuiti for **San Nicolò ❻** (daily 9am–1pm), the largest and eeriest church in Sicily. Work was curtailed by the 1693 earthquake and the church was later abandoned, incomplete. The huge adjoining Benedictine monastery is now part of the university. Guided visits (Mon–Fri hourly 9am–5pm, Sat–Sun 9am–noon) reveal cloisters, a hanging garden and the remains of a Roman house.

From Piazza Dante head east to **Via Etnea**, the main shopping street. Going north, towards Etna, cross **Piazza Stesicoro**, with its **Anfiteatro Romano ❼**, the remains of the largest amphitheatre in Sicily. Carry on to **Villa Bellini**, delightful gardens where you can retreat from the bustle.

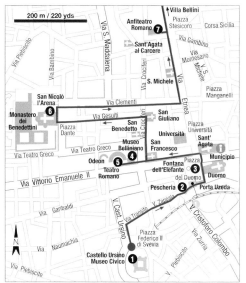

The Teatro Greco hosts a series of events throughout the year

TAORMINA

Taormina is Sicily's glitziest and most dramatically situated resort, perched on a hill overlooking the coast and Mount Etna. Stroll through the centre, soaking up the views, or hike up the hill to Castelmola. A performance at the Teatro Greco makes a memorable end to the day.

DISTANCE: Walk in Taormina, 3km (2 miles), optional 2km (1.25-mile) walk to Castelmola
TIME: A half-day walk
START/END: Corso Umberto I. Optional excursions to Mazzarò, Isola Bella and Castelmola
POINTS TO NOTE: Cars should be left in hotel car parks, or in car parks below the centre. Lumbi Parking on the approach road has a shuttle service to the centre or Mazzarò. Parking in Mazzarò on the coast has a cable-car link to Taormina. Parking is expensive (around €25 for 24 hours). A scenic rail route runs along the coast to Taormina's Giardini station, with a 10-minute bus ride to the top of the town. To avoid the worst of the crowds, see the Teatro Greco at 9am or at the end of the day. In summer, book tickets for events at the Greek theatre (www. taormina-arte.com).

It is no surprise that the Greeks and Romans took advantage of the per-fect setting on the east of the island and built a theatre here. Taormina is the royal box in one of the grandest of nature's theatres. The resort stands perched on the lower of a descending series of crags nearly 300m (1,000ft) above the coast. There are spectacular views in all directions, by day and night: to the south Mount Etna looms, to the north there are views across sweeping bays and the dark hills of Calabria.

Taormina makes an enticing base for excursions – though be warned that midsummer is best avoided. Spring is a wonderful time to visit, given the mild weather and profusion of pink blossom. But don't expect empty streets – the town lives off tourism and from early spring to late autumn it's abuzz with visitors.

The centre comprises a main street and a maze of steep, narrow alleys, mostly reserved for pedestrians. It is still very charming in a restored and stagey way, with colourful window boxes, lemon and orange groves, and alfresco cafés on small squares.

Busy Piazza Aprile

THE CENTRE

Most visitors enter Taormina at **Porta Messina ❶**, the gateway leading into the pedestrianised **Corso Umberto I**, the normally packed thoroughfare that bisects the town. Weather-beaten palazzi have been converted into craft shops, designer boutiques, jewellers and bars, while luxury emporia display bottled peppers, candied fruit, marzipan animals and fresh kumquats. Side streets reveal balconies hung with geraniums and bougainvillaea.

Palazzo Corvaja

At the east end of the Corso on Piazza Vittorio Emanuele II, the tourist office occupies **Palazzo Corvaja ❷**, a historic mansion with a crenellated Arab tower. In the chamber on the first floor the Sicilian 'Parliament' met in 1411, now it is home to folkloric exhibits of the **Museo Siciliano di Arte e Tradizioni Populari** (Sicilian Museum of Art and Popular Traditions). From here, walk uphill to the **Odeon Romano ❸**, a Roman concert auditorium almost concealed by the charming church of **Santa Caterina**.

The Greek Theatre

From here follow the flow along the gentle slope of Via Teatro Greco to Taormina's most famous site, the **Teatro Greco ❹** (daily 9am–1 hour before sunset; charge). The setting, overlooking smouldering Etna, the coast and Calabrian mountains, is pure drama. The theatre was carved out of the hillside by the Greeks in the 3rd century BC and was later enlarged by the Romans. While in Greek theatres sea and sky were the natural backdrop, the Romans preferred proscenium arches. They added a double portico and colonnades behind the stage, closing off views of sea and mountains. The attention of spectators was instead focused on the arena, which under the Romans became a circus exclusively for gladiatorial combat. Today the theatre makes a magnificent setting for drama, ballet, music and cinema (from June to October).

Naumachie and Piazza IX Aprile

From theatrical heights walk back down Via Teatro

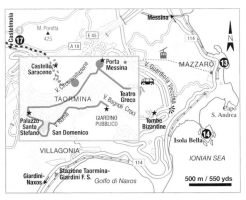

Concert at the Teatro Greco

Greco and pause for a drink in the busy piazza before re-entering the fray on Corso Umberto I. The first passageway on the left leads to the **Naumachie ❺**, a hybrid construction which began as a vaulted cistern connected to the city baths but became a Greek nymphaeum (a monument consecrated to nymphs) and Roman gymnasium. The ancient arched buttress walls remain, propping up the Corso.

Piazza IX Aprile ❻, halfway down the Corso, has panoramic views of Etna and the sea. **Sant'Agostino**, the austere 15th-century church on the square, has been converted into a cosy library, while the 17th-century **San Giuseppe** has an ornate rococo stucco interior. Continue along the Corso, passing beneath the **Porta di Mezzo**, or clock-tower, into the **Borgo Medievale**, the oldest quarter of the town.

Piazza del Duomo

Piazza del Duomo ❼ is a popular meeting place and home to the crenellated **Cattedrale di San Nicolò** (daily 9am–8pm). **Vecchia Taormina**, see ①, is a good spot for lunch. From the square, stepped alleys lead up to Piazza del Carmine and the **Badia Vecchia ❽**, a battlemented 15th-century abbey with splendid views and housing the local **Museo Archeologico** (closed for

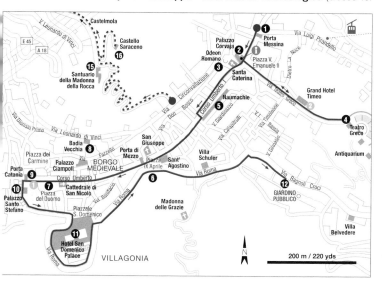

Painter on Piazza Aprile   *Inside Taormina's arts museum*

restoration). The Corso ends at **Porta Catania** ❾, the archway that matches the Porta Messina gate.

Down the steps, off Piazza Sant'Antonio, the **Palazzo Santo Stefano** ❿ is a gracious ducal palace with a concoction of Norman windows, lava-stone cornices and a lacy frieze of delicate wood inlay – an Arab legacy. From here the road leads to **San Domenico** ⓫, a 15th-century monastery, used by the Germans in World War II, then converted into a luxury hotel.

GIARDINO PUBBLICO

Stroll back along the winding Via Roma, which brings you to the exotic **Giardino Pubblico** ⓬ (also called Villa Comunale; daily dawn–dusk; free). The hanging gardens, dotted with pagoda-style follies, tropical plants and with a sea-view terrace, were the creation of Florence Trevelyan, an eccentric Scots aristocrat who had to leave Britain after an affair with the Prince of Wales, the future Edward VII.

TAORMINA BY NIGHT

A stroll after dark through the centre of Taormina is an essential experience. The Catalan Gothic facades are eerily illuminated, the squares tinged pink in the moonlight. The main form of evening entertainment is the *passeggiata* along Corso Umberto I – the shops close only when everyone goes home. From Piazza IX Aprile you may see Mount Etna's fiery cone. For cocktails, join the fashionistas at the **Hotel San Domenico Palace**. Or for less exclusive nightlife a drive down to Giardini-Naxos offers waterfront strolls, seafood bars and discotheques.

For fine dining, you could opt for the **Grand Hotel Timeo Restaurant**, see ❷, near the Greek Theatre, but be pre-

Catering for all

Taormina was first publicised by a trio of Germans: a writer, a painter and a photographer. In 1787 the writer Goethe pronounced Taormina 'a patch of paradise on earth'. The artist Otto Geleng later drew visitors to the island with his romantic landscapes. Von Gleden spent 50 years from 1880 photographing nude shepherd boys, emulating bucolic poems. Draped in exotic leopard skins, Taormina's lithe peasants scandalised Sicilian society and made Taormina a gay mecca.

This louche image runs in parallel with Taormina's reputation as Sicily's earliest, smartest winter resort. A 'fashionable loafing place', it was patronised by leisured Edwardians. D.H. Lawrence had a villa here in the early 1920s, and during the 1940s such luminaries as Gloria Vanderbilt, Marlene Dietrich, Rita Hayworth and Joan Crawford were part of the social scene. The terraced town still attracts a chic crowd and remains Sicily's most gay-friendly resort.

View up to Castelmola

pared for a bill that matches the spectacular views.

MAZZARÒ AND BELLA ISOLA

Unless it's peak season, consider an afternoon on the pebbly, well-equipped beaches of **Mazzarò** ⑬, situated below Taormina. The cable car (charge) from Via Luigi Pirandello runs every 15 minutes.

Take a rowing boat beyond the Capo Sant'Andrea for the lovely cove with two beaches (also accessible on foot) and the tiny **Isola Bella** ⑭, which has become a marine reserve, popular with divers. The 'Roman Temple' shipwreck dive, 26m (85ft) down, reveals marble columns which were destined for a temple in Taormina.

CASTELMOLA

If a hike up the hill appeals, take the path to the **Santuario della Madonna della Rocca** ⑮ above Taormina, and just above it the ruins of the **Castello Saraceno** ⑯. The walk starts at Via Circonvallazione in Taormina, with a steep path signed 'Castel Taormina/Madonna della Rocca'.

Have a cooling drink at the Castello Saraceno, admire the views and, if it's not too hot, carry on up to **Castelmola** ⑰ (around 50 minutes), a hamlet with a ruined castle perched on a limestone peak. (You can also get here by car or bus – it's about 5km/3 miles.)

Castelmola is quite touristy but worth the climb for the panorama. Try a glass of *vino alla mandorla* (almond wine), the sweet local tipple. **Antico Caffè San Giorgio**, see ❸, in the square, has the finest views.

Food and Drink

❶ VECCHIA TAORMINA

Vico Ebrei 3; tel: 0942 625 589; L and D Thur–Tue, but closed L July–Aug; €
An excellent pizzeria in the heart of town with a wood-burning oven and courtyard seating.

❷ GRAND HOTEL TIMEO RESTAURANT

Via Teatro Greco 40; tel: 0942 23801; L and D daily; www.grandhoteltimeo.com; €€€€
Dreamy fine dining framed by a timeless panorama in which Etna and Capo Taormina are the stars. The food mixes island recipes (for pasta or desserts) and gourmet classics (risotto).

❸ ANTICO CAFFÈ SAN GIORGIO

Piazza S. Antonio, Castelmola; tel: 0942 28228; daily 7.30am–midnight; €
Follow in the footsteps of Churchill, Rockefeller and Pope John Paul II (to name a few), sipping almond wine on the terrace and soaking up stupendous views of Taormina and the Gulf of Naxos. Rustic antipasti and granite are also on offer at this historic inn. Reservations advisable.

Mighty Etna

EXPLORING ETNA: FOOTHILLS AND ASCENT

Start at the stunning Alcántara Gorge, skirt the volcanic foothills of Mount Etna and visit black lava villages in the jaws of the volcano. Add another day or half-day for the ascent to the main crater.

DISTANCE: 187km/116 miles (137km/85.5 miles if returning to Catania)
TIME: Foothills drive: one day; ascent: half or one day
START: Taormina
END: Catania or Taormina
POINTS TO NOTE: Choose a clear day for views of Etna. Take swimming gear and sturdy shoes for the Alcántara Gorge. If climbing Etna you will need warm clothes, walking shoes or boots, hat, sunglasses, sunscreen and water. Jacket and boots can be rented. Independent hikers should take advice before setting off. For trekking companies with professional local guides contact Etna Experience (www.etnaexperience.com) or Guide Etna Nord (www.guidetnanord.com). Climbs to the crater are subject to weather conditions and volcanic activity and can be cancelled without warning. Tour agencies in Catania and Etna offer half- or full-day 4-wheel-drive and trekking excursions.

Etna is Europe's largest and most active volcano, and it makes its present felt. Whether snow-capped, charcoal-coloured or partially swathed in mist, it is visible from afar. *Mongibello*, the local name for Etna, comes from the Arabic for mountain. The native Siculi tribes believed that Adranus, the god of fire, fashioned the volcano, while to the Greeks, Etna was Vulcan's forge, moulding black magic from incandescent magma. To modern Sicilians, Mongibello is sacred, beneficent yet pitiless, the gold of fertility and the god of destruction. 'Etna has taken back my orchard!' cried a farmer in 1992, as a tide of molten lava engulfed his land.

The eruption in 693 BC reached the coast, while the 1669 explosion wiped out Catania. The lava took eight years to cool. The last decade or so has seen a flurry of seismic activity. In 2002 it destroyed the ski lifts, cable car and tourist complex at the Rifugio Sapienza southern gateway, and intense eruptions have continued sporadically ever since, with one particularly dramatic-looking one in 2012. Notwithstanding,

Gole dell'Alcántara

over 20 percent of Sicilians still choose to live on these risky slopes.

On clear days the views are stupendous. In winter (and often until late April or May) Etna is snow-capped. At the lower levels, the potassium- and phosphate-rich soil is ideal for citrus groves, above them vines and olives flourish, then higher up broom and prickly pear give way to pine groves. Above the tree line lies a moonscape scarred by clinker.

The Alcántara Gorge

From Taormina drive south to Giardini-Naxos and take the SS185 inland. After 15km (9 miles), visit the popular **Gole dell'Alcántara ❶** (Apr–Oct daily 8am–sunset; www.terralcantara.it; charge for lift), a stunning 20m (66ft) deep gorge. The pitted river canyon was created by the collision of volcanic magma and the cooling water of the river, the impact throwing up lavic prisms in warped shapes. A lift leads down to the grey-green river and the so-called beach, where in summer you can paddle in the icy waters or hire waders and wetsuits to explore further. Beyond are rapids that can be explored on guided rafting, kayaking and canyoning tours (www.acquaterra.it).

Castiglione di Sicilia

Beyond the gorge, **Francavilla di Sicilia ❷** is set in a fertile valley of citrus plantations, with King Roger's ruined castle occupying a lone mound. Follow signs up to **Castiglione di Sicilia ❸**, an atmospheric village perched on a crag. It retains some Greek ramparts but is essentially a bastion of basalt churches and quiet, medieval alleys. The ruined **Norman Castle**, destined to become a wine-tasting centre, dominates the valley, with lovely views over red-tiled roofs to citrus groves beyond. Enjoy an early lunch and the panorama at **Belvedere d'Alcántara**, see ❶.

Randazzo

Enjoy the views of Etna as you wind south to join the SS120. Turn right here for **Randazzo ❹**, the most coherent medieval town on the northern slopes of Etna. During Swabian times this was a cool summer retreat for the royal court. Although lying in the jaws of Etna, the town survived numerous eruptions, but as the Nazis' last stand in Sicily, suffered from Allied bombs. What remains is a tribute to the medieval rivalry between Randazzo's three communities: Latins, Greeks and Lombards settled in different parishes, and each of their crenellated churches became the cathedral for a three-year term. The Catholics triumphed, and **Santa Maria** on **Via Umberto I** is now the cathedral. This main street contains the severe Swabian summer palace and other symbols of Randazzo's past role as a royal city. At the far end the **Chiesa San Martino** is graced by a 13th-century banded lava and limestone bell tower, matched by a grey and white stone Baroque facade. Close

Randazzo   *Alcántara blooms*

by is the **Castello Svevo**, a medieval castle and Bourbon prison, now the **Museo Vagliasindi** (daily 10am–1pm, 3–7pm; charge), with archaeological finds and Sicilian puppets.

Follow one of the alleys to the city walls and views of ruined battlements beyond, then consider lunch at **San Giorgio e Il Drago**, see ❼, a rustic-style restaurant near the church of Santa

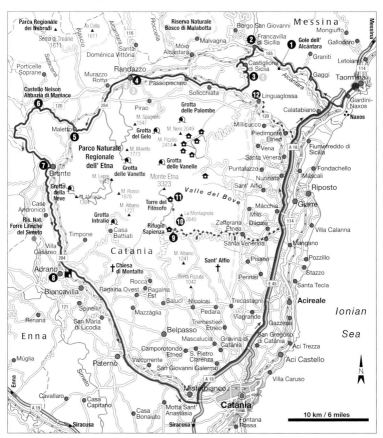

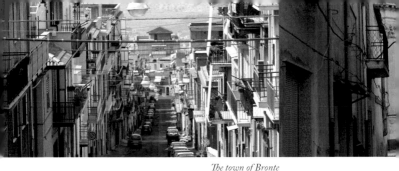

The town of Bronte

Maria, or the **Trattoria Veneziano**, see ❶, 2km (1.25 miles) out of town, off the SS120 going east.

Castello Nelson

Continue on the circular route, branching left onto the S284 south of Randazzo. **Maletto** ❺ further south offers views of recent lava flows. From here follow signs for **Maniace** and **Castello Nelson** ❻ (9am–1pm, 2.30–5pm, until 7pm in summer; charge).

Founded by Count Roger, this is best-known as the one-time estate of Admiral Horatio Nelson. It was presented to him by Ferdinand IV when he was created Duke of Bronte in 1799. Nelson's descendants lived here until 1981 and, although the estate was broken up, Nelson memorabilia remains, from paintings of sea battles to the admiral's port decanter. The Benedictine abbey was destroyed by the 1693 earthquake but retains the late Norman chapel with original wooden ceiling and a portal with fine carvings. Don't expect a castle – it's more like an English manor house.

Bronte

Follow signs for **Bronte** ❼, taking you onto the SS120 and SP165. The road winds through walnut and chestnut groves, then, nearing Bronte, plantations of pistachio trees. These produce 80 percent of Italy's crop. The pistachios, harvested biannually, are used in pasta dishes, patisserie and ice creams, and a pistachio festival takes place annually in the first 10 days of October. Pistachios apart, Bronte is unremarkable: a rather shabby town sandwiched between two lava flows.

Adrano

Bronte gives way to alpine plains, scrubland and lava-encrusted slopes – relics of the 1985 eruption. The SS284 takes you south to **Adrano** ❽. Set on Etna's southwest slopes, this market town was once the Greek city of Adranon, and was celebrated for its sanctuary to Adranus, the Siculi god of fire. Its outskirts are dotted with Greek masonry, matched by sections of city wall beyond Via Buglio. The town's battered charm lies in the busy **Piazza Umberto** with the massive **Norman Castle**, rebuilt by Roger I and the Aragonese, and the neighbouring **Chiesa Madre**, a much-restored church of Norman origin incorporating basalt columns from an ancient Greek temple.

Unless you are hiking from Nicolosi or taking the cable car from Rifugio Sapienza, follow the SS284 Catania road from Adrano which feeds into the autostrada. From here it is only half an hour's drive back to Taormina along the fast A18, allowing perhaps time for a sunset cocktail overlooking Etna's fireworks.

ASCENT OF ETNA

Be advised by the experts because, depending on volcanic activity, Etna can be a damp squib or the most dramatic

Street view of Adrano

Rifugio Sapienza

memory of your stay. Without a guide, suitably clad hikers can clamber about at their own risk up to a certain altitude, currently around 3,000m (9850ft), 323m (1060ft) short of Etna's height. The two principal approaches are Etna Nord (north) and Etna Sud (south).

SOUTHERN APPROACH – RIFUGIO SAPIENZA

The simplest way of seeing the crater is the cable-car excursion from **Rifugio Sapienza ❾** (at 1920m/6,300ft), which also includes an optional guided drive and walk to the summit. From Taormina it is a 60km (37.5-mile) drive: take the A18 autostrada, exit at Giarre and head west via Santa Venerina and Zafferana Etna. Alternatively there is a bus (Mon–Sat) departing from Catania's Stazione Centrale at 8.15am and returning at 4.30pm, and an extra one at 11am in August. The Rifugio has a live TV feed from the top, showing the conditions, so you can check before departing. The **cable car** (Apr–Nov 9am–5.30pm, Dec–Mar 9am–3.45pm; www.funivia etna.com; charge), used by skiers in winter, takes you to **La Montagnola ❿** (2,640m/8,200ft), where you can stop for coffee and admire the views. From here there is the option of a 4-wheel-drive minibus with guide (Mar–Nov, €59 including cable car) to **Torre del Filósofo ⓫** at 2,920m. The journey, including cable car and jeep, takes around two and a half hours.

By foot

The energetic can go all the way up from the Rifugio Sapienza by foot. It takes around four hours to get up – faster, of course, coming down. Less challenging is the cable car and walking the rest of the way (around 2km/1.25 miles). For other mountain treks from the south, visit www.etnaguide.com.

NORTHERN APPROACH – PIANO PROVENZANA

The gateway to Etna's northern slopes is **Piano Provenzana**, a ski resort 16km (10 miles) southwest of **Linguaglossa ⓬**. There is no public transport, so you

Volcano railway

The alternative to a car tour is the quaint Circumetnea Railway (www.circumetnea. it) which skirts the lower slopes of Etna. This single-track rail route, which has been in existence since 1894, is a leisurely 114km (71-mile) journey, starting in Catania, taking in Adrano, Bronte and Randazzo and returning to the coast at Giarre-Riposto south of Taormina.

This is a wonderful trip and excellent value, affording fine views of the fertile lower slopes as well as Etna itself. Depending on the timetable and sections open you will have time to stop off at one of the stations. Randazzo is the most appealing town en route. Note that trains do not run on Sundays.

Descending Etna

will need to drive. (From Taormina exit the A18 autostrada at Fiumefreddo and follow SS120 towards Randazzo for Linguaglossa. From there follow the mountain road to Piano Provenzana). From May to October S.T.A.R (tel: 095 371 333, or starct@tin.it) operate 4-wheel-drive minibuses with a guide up to a height of 2800m (9186ft). The climb on foot is a 6–7 hour round trip (contact www.guidetnanord.com).

What to see

While it would be foolish to expect apocalyptic eruptions and a river of molten lava, Etna is fascinating in its many moods and offers plenty to see, from the purplish-brown heaps of volcanic rubble to the comical decapitated cones and gaping lava mouths. Around the cones, the encrusted lava is black, mauve, grey or red, depending on age. If you're lucky you may see a glowing red crater, the belching of sulphurous vapours, a shower of sparks or gaseous explosions.

Etna's eruptive mode shows little sign of abating, and locals continue to make the most of their asset. The glittering red cone is visible from Catania during the day, while visitors in Taormina are virtually guaranteed a nightly spectacle of molten bombs shooting from Etna's cones.

The German writer Goethe was overwhelmed by the Sicilians' success at 'selling everything the volcano vomits'. The fruitful exploitation of Etna continues, and few visitors leave the volcano without lumps of rock, lava ashtrays or little lava animals.

Food and Drink

① BELVEDERE D'ALCÁNTARA

Via Abbate Coniglio 44, Castiglione di Sicilia; tel: 0942 984 037; L and D Tue–Sun Apr–Oct; www.belvederedalcantara.it; €

Come for panoramic views of the Alcántara valley, good home cooking and prices that are half those of Taormina. The four-course menu at €18 (wine included) will typically include antipasti full of local flavours, house macaroni, rabbit and home-made desserts.

② SAN GIORGIO E IL DRAGO

Piazza San Giorgio 28, Randazzo; tel: 095 923 972; L and D Wed–Mon, closed three weeks in January; €€

The good-value St George and the Dragon offers pasta with funghi or wild herbs from Etna, followed by meaty regional mains such as rabbit with caper and olive sauce.

③ TRATTORIA VENEZIANO

Km 187 SS120, Contrada Arena, Randazzo; tel: 0957 991 353; www.ristoranteveneziano.it; L and D Tue–Sat; L Sun; €€

Just out of town, this is a modern restaurant with pretensions, but it has tasty regional dishes. Mushrooms from the slopes of Etna are a speciality. Try them with rigatoni pasta or with rabbit or wild boar.

View over the Aeolian Islands from Vulcano

THE AEOLIAN ISLANDS

Shaped by wind and fire, these tiny volcanic islands rise up from indigo seas off Sicily's north coast. Though increasingly popular with visitors, the archipelago still offers a real sense of adventure. Base yourself in Lípari for two to three days and ferry-hop to explore the smaller islands.

DISTANCE: From Milazzo to Lípari, then to the other islands: 356 km (221 miles)

TIME: 3 days

START: Milazzo

END: Lípari

POINTS TO NOTE: For information on how to get to the islands, see page 132. Cars are not allowed access in summer unless you are staying for at least a week, but vehicles can be left in private garages in Milazzo. If you only have a day to spare, consider a Panarea and Strómboli excursion (www.minicrociereisoleeolie.com), leaving Milazzo at noon, returning at 11pm, enabling you to watch Strómboli erupt at night. If climbing the Gran Cratere on Vulcano, take water, stout shoes, hat and sunscreen. For Strómboli hiking boots and clothes can be rented on the island.

The Greeks named the islands after Aeolus, the hospitable god of the winds who lived on Lípari and gave Ulysses a wineskin of winds to guide his ship back home to the Greek island of Ithaca. But even Aeolus, assuming he was more than a myth, is recent compared to the first settlers who arrived in Lípari in the 5th millennium BC. Prior to their arrival a volcano on Lípari had erupted, spewing huge quantities of magma which solidified to become obsidian. The hard black volcanic glass was much prized for crafting sharp tools and the island grew prosperous by trading them in the Mediterranean.

The islands were regarded as remote and inhospitable until around 50 years ago. Today these Unesco World Heritage dots in the Tyrrhenian Sea are inundated from mid-July to the end of August, but they are a delight in spring, early summer and autumn. Winter, when boats are often cancelled and you can get stranded on the islands, is best avoided.

Lípari (36 sq km/14 sq miles) is the largest and the hub of the archipelago. With its choice of accommodation, excursions and water sports, this makes the best base. The tours below take you to smouldering Vulcano, spectacular Stróm-

boli, chic Panarea and laidback Salina, but if staying longer you might also consider seeing Filicudi and Alicudi, remote rocky outcrops at the western end of the archipelago, with wild unspoilt scenery.

LÍPARI

Hydrofoils from Milazzo take around an hour and most stop at Vulcano en route. Ferries and hydrofoils dock at Marina Lunga, the bustling main port of **Lípari** ❶. From here take the café- and shop-lined **Corso Vittorio Emanuele**, where the *passeggiata* seems to take place most of the day. Tiny *vici* or alleys, crammed with potted plants and Vespas, lead up from this main *corso*, linking with the only other main road, the Via Garibaldi. Liparí town is the main attraction of the island, but away from the town there are mountains to climb, hot springs and bright white hillsides and beaches of pumice. Cars, scooters or bikes can be hired, or there are public buses that do a full circuit of the island from June to September. The coast, with its multicoloured cliffs, clear indigo waters, caves and grottoes is best explored on a boat excursion.

The Citadel
From Via Garibaldi the **Via Concordato**, a wide cobbled stairway, leads up to the splendid **Citadel ❹**, built by the Spanish in the 16th century and absorbing a Greek tower and walls from the 4th century BC. The Norman cathedral was burnt down by Barbarossa in 1544 and the church you see today, the **Cattedrale di San Bartolomeo**, crowning the Citadel, is largely Baroque, but retains Norman vaults and cloister.

Archaeological Museum
Over the centuries, volcanic ash, spread by the Mediterranean mistral, formed 9m (29.5ft) strata on the citadel. A huge, painstaking excavation in the 1950s–70s yielded evidence of continuous occupation from the 4th millennium BC. The outstanding **Museo Archeologico Eoliano ❸** (Mon–Sat 9am–1pm, 3–6pm, Sun 9am–1pm, by reservation only in winter; charge), in buildings either side of the cathedral, holds a treasure trove of prehistoric and classical artefacts found on Lípari and other parts of southern Italy.

The former Bishop's Palace houses the Neolithic and Bronze Age exhibits, including many tools crafted in obsidian. The Classical section displays burial urns, decorated vases and an extraordinary rich collection of 100 terracotta theatrical masks discovered in tombs from the 4th to 3rd century BC.

Marina Corta
Via Garibaldi drops down to **Marina Corta**, a colourful and busy little port, with small boats coming and going. Survey the scene from an alfresco table or have a leisurely typically Aeolian lunch in a lovely setting at nearby **La Nassa**, see ❶.

Mud bath on Vulcano

VULCANO

Vulcano ❷ is home of the god of fire. Excursion boats depart regularly from Marina Corta (try bargaining off season), fishermen offer scenic trips in summer or hydrofoils/ferries depart from Marina Lunga.

On arrival you're greeted by sulphurous odours coming from the smouldering **Gran Cratere**, but don't be put off by the fumes – the volcano has been dormant since 1890. The hour's hike up (charge for the path) is not too challenging but can be very hot. Allow time for walking around the peak and admiring the dramatic views.

The volcano supplies the island with its other main activity: thermal mud baths, said to cure skin disorders and rheumatic pains. Below the crater you can wallow in the warm *fanghi* (7am–11pm summer, 8am–5pm off season; charge), shallow pools of thick mud, then clean up in the thermally heated seawater pool, or head on to **Spiaggia Sabbia Nera**, a big sweep of black volcanic beach with red-hot sand where you can take a refreshing dip and admire the sunset.

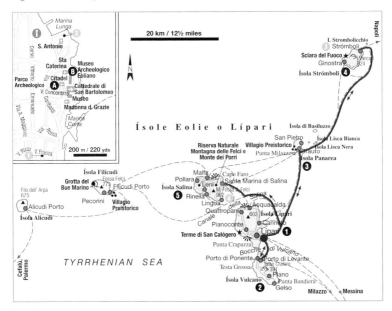

DIRECTORY

Hand-picked hotels and restaurants to suit all budgets and tastes, organised by area, plus select nightlife listings, an alphabetical listing of practical information, a language guide and an overview of the best books and films to give you a flavour of the island.

Grand Hotel Timeo, Taormina

ACCOMMODATION

Sicily has plentiful accommodation, with prices similar to the mainland. The choice ranges from grand hotels in Palermo, Catania and Taormina and stylish boutique hotels to simple B&Bs and rooms on farms. Accommodation in the interior is thinner on the ground, although there is a swathe of special hotels in and around Siracusa, Ragusa, Módica and Scicli. Book ahead for popular resorts such as Taormina, Cefalù and Siracusa, especially during Easter and summer. The same applies to hotels on the offshore islands. Many resorts close in winter; some hotels and *agriturismi* insist on half or full board during high season.

Agriturismi or farm stays have improved dramatically and are generally delightful and good value. Some of these might be rural estates, country houses or rural apartments rather than farms.

> Price for a double room including breakfast during high season:
>
> €€€€ = over €300
> €€€ = €180–300
> €€ = €100–180
> € = under €100
>
> In line with Rome, hotels in some of the larger cities now charge a hotel tax of €2–4 per person for the first five consecutive nights.

If you want to make an early morning start up Etna, Rifugio Sapienza (tel: 095 915 321) is a simple chalet with direct access to the cable car. Set up at 1900m (6,230ft), it can be cold, but these days the *rifugio* has decent heating, plus a café and restaurant. Tourists arrive for the cable car mid-morning, but by this time you'll be way ahead of the pack. Villa rental is now big business thanks to foreign villa owners and design-conscious locals.

Palermo

BB22
Palazzo Pantelleria, Largo Cavalieri di Malta 22; tel: 091 326 214; www.bb22.it; €€
This unique B&B has an excellent location in the historic centre, tucked behind San Domenico and close to the Vucciria Market. The seven guest rooms are handsomely furnished with plenty of designer chic.

Centrale Palace
Corso Vittorio Emanuele 327; tel: 091 336 666; www.centralepalacehotel.it; €€€€
A luxurious, well-restored hotel, Centrale Palace exudes a charm lacking in many other Palermo hotels. Its location, close to the Quattro Canti crossroads, is central. Breakfast is served on the terrace with panoramic view over the old town roofs.

Bar at the Villa Igiea Hilton

Conte Federico

Via dei Biscottari 4; tel: 091 651 1881;
www.contefederico.com; €€

Run by a Palermitan count and his opera-singing Austrian wife, this palace in the heart of town offers an intriguing insight into Sicilian life. The apartments, all with private bathrooms, lead off the 17th-century courtyard.

Excelsior Hilton

Via Marchese Ugo 3; tel: 091 790 9001;
www.excelsiorpalermo.it; €€€€

Refurbished in elegant 19th-century style, this established hotel overlooks a park in the chic, new part of Palermo, but is still within reasonable distance of the historic centre. Rooms vary considerably, so you may wish to view before booking. Friendly staff.

Grand Hotel des Palmes

Via Roma 398; tel: 091 602 8111;
www.grandhoteldespalmes.com;
€€–€€€€

This splendidly faded landmark is in a good location for exploring the historic centre and elegant new Palermo. Belle Epoque flourishes remain, as does the Art Nouveau lobby. Mafia and musical associations abound – Wagner completed *Parsifal* here in 1882.

Grand Hotel Piazza Borsa

Via dei Cartari 18; tel: 091 320 075;
www.piazzaborsa.it; €€€–€€€€

Opened in 2010, this atmospheric hotel in the heart of the city combines a for-mer monastery, church and cloisters as well as several ancient palazzi, including the former stock exchange. Among the highlights are a spa, spacious bedrooms, a bar in the cloisters, a winter garden and a gourmet restaurant in an Art Nouveau setting.

Orientale

Via Maqueda 26; tel: 091 616 5727;
www.albergoorientale.191.it; €

This is an excellent budget option, just 100m/yds from Stazione Centrale. Rooms are located in an atmospheric 18th-century palace built around an arcaded courtyard, but only half of them are en suite.

Palazzo Sitano

Via Vittorio Emanuele 114; tel: 091 611 9880; www.hotelpalazzositano.it; €€–€€€

This stylish contemporary hotel is close to regenerated Piazza Marina with a good choice of restaurants and bars. Slick rooms are fitted out in black, browns and beiges, while the excellent breakfast is served in a lovely, light-filled room.

Villa Igiea Hilton

Salita Belmonte 43; tel: 091 631 2111;
www.villa-igiea.com; €€€–€€€€

Set out of town in Acquasanta, on cliffs above the bay, this is Palermo's most prestigious hotel. Once a villa built by the Florio dynasty (of tuna and wine fame), it has now been restored to full Art Nouveau splendour. Facilities

The Orientale in Palermo

include leisurely trips on the villa boat, a beach club and a shuttle bus service to Palermo.

Mondello

Mondello Palace
Viale Principe di Scalea; tel: 091 450 001; www.mondellopalace hotel.it; €€€–€€€€

Palermo's favourite seaside retreat is the setting for this luxurious hotel. On the seafront and surrounded by a garden, it offers good-sized rooms, most with sea views. Facilities include a private beach, swimming pool, restaurant and bar. Reserve well ahead in summer.

Splendid La Torre
Via Piano Gallo 11; tel: 091 450 222; www.latorre.com; €€

A modern hotel on the rocky point of the bay at the quieter end of Mondello Lido. Own beach, pool and tennis courts, and sea or garden views from the rooms. There is also a restaurant serving delicious fish dishes.

Cefalù

Baia del Capitano
Contrada Mazzaforno; tel: 0921 420 003/005; www.baiadelcapitano.it; €€€

This modern hotel has a lovely setting in an olive grove about 5km (3 miles) west of Cefalù. The more expensive rooms have terrace gardens and sea views. A nearby beach is accessible on foot or by free hotel shuttle, and the hotel has its own swimming pool.

Kalura
Via Vincenzo Cavallaro 13, Caldura; tel: 0921 421 354; www.hotel-kalura.com; €€€

Ensconced in Mediterranean foliage, 3km (2 miles) from Cefalù, the family-run Kalura offers clean and spacious rooms, most with a terrace and sea view. This is a family-friendly place with a spacious pool and children's pool, private beach, mountain bikes to hire and water sports nearby.

Scopello

La Tavernetta
Via Armando Diaz 3; tel: 0924 541 129; www.albergolatavernetta.it; €

This friendly little hotel in a pretty coastal village near the Roserva dello Zingaro was restored in 2012. Most of the rooms have balconies and sea views. Half board, which is good value, is compulsory in high season.

La Vera Sicilia
Tel: 091 549338 or 340 550 2032; www.valmassvacanze.weekly.com; €

A Sicilian-German couple own these two apartments in Scopello – check the website to see which appeal. Cosy Giardino del Re, which opens onto a garden once owned by Ferdiant IV, is one of the best. The apartment is a 10-minute walk to the sea.

Trápani

Ai Lumi
Corso Vittorio Emanuele 71; tel: 0923 540 922; www.ailumi.it; €

Breakfast with a view　　　　　　　　　　　*Trápani beach*

In the historic heart of town, this is an atmospheric, family-run B&B within an 18th-century palazzo. Rooms with kitchenette, private bathroom and Wi-Fi surround a splendid courtyard. It has the distinct advantage of being in the same building (and under the same management) as the best restaurant in town (see page 52), with a 15 percent discount for B&B guests.

Cortile Antico

Vicolo Compagni (traversa via
Poeta Calvino); tel: 0923 362989;
www.cortileantico.com; €

An old building arranged around an ancient courtyard is the setting of this small hotel, offering one-room and two-room apartments in the heart of the city. The patio has a local flavour, recalling old Sicily, while the interior is modern and comfortable, with design furniture and a variety of services and accessories.

La Gancia Residence

Piazza Mercato del Pesce; tel: 0923 438
060; www.lagancia.com; €€

Just on the sea, this welcoming residence offers splendid views of the Mediterranean. Formerly a Carmelite convent, it was recently restored and turned into modern a modern hotel, offering delightful self-catered apartments, each with its own with kitchenette, telephone, internet connection and fine furniture. Some of the apartments have marvellous terraces. Minimum stay: 4 nights.

B&B Porta delle Botteghelle

Via Serisso 31; tel 0923 19 86 111;
www.portadellebotteghelle.it; €

Part of a building dating from the second half of the 8th century, this small bed-and-breakfast has been fully renovated and equipped with modern comforts and technology. The rooms are simple but full of character, with have wooden ceilings and design furniture, and the hotel is conveniently located a few steps away from the harbour.

Erice

Elimo

Via Vittorio Emanuele 75; tel: 0923 869 377;
www.hotelelimo.it; €€

This cosy 17th-century palazzo in the old town is a perfect retreat from the mists of mountain-top Erice, the ideal place from which to savour the citadel's other worldly atmosphere. Public areas are dotted with antiques and modern art, and there are lovely views from the rooms and roof terrace.

Moderno

Via Vittorio Emanuele 67;
tel: 0923 869 300; www.hotel
modernoerice.it; €€

The excellent restaurant, renowned for its fish couscous, draws tourists and locals to the Moderno. Those who stay on enjoy a well-run, intimate hotel. Furnishings include antiques, country pieces and the hand-woven rugs for which Erice is famous.

The Kempinski Giardino di Costanza near Salemi

Mazara del Vallo

Kempinski Giardino di Costanza

Via Salemi, Giardino di Costanza; tel: 0923 675 000; www.gdcresort.com; €€€€

Situated only 7km (4.3 miles) from the historic town of Salemi, this luxurious hotel is part of the German Kempinski chain. Surrounded by olive groves and vineyards, the resort has two pools (inside and out), spa, tennis, children's programme, fine restaurant and suites with jacuzzis.

Mahara Hotel

Lungomare San Vito 3; tel: 0923 673 800; www.maharahotel.it; €€

This great-value four-star hotel on the seafront occupies an old Marsala wine warehouse. Rooms have views of the gardens and pool or the seafront. Facilities include a wellness centre, good fish restaurant and free shuttle bus to the beach.

Selinunte

Villa Mimosa

La Rocchetta, Castelvetrano; tel: 0924 44583; www.villamimosasicily.com; €

This charmingly rustic villa is owned by Englishwoman Jackie Sirimanne, who has lived in Sicily for years and knows the island like the back of her hand. Rooms decked out with floral fabrics and original prints open onto a terrace and garden of jasmine and citrus trees. Each room has a kitchenette, but you can also dine *en famille* (give 24 hours' notice).

Agrigento

Colleverde Park

Passeggiata Archeologica; tel: 0922 29555; www.colleverdehotel.it. €€

This quiet and welcoming hotel is situated at the start of Strada Panoramica. The 48 rooms are modern and the lush park surrounding the hotel offers lovely views of the Valley of Temples. It also houses a reasonable restaurant serving seasonal dishes.

Foresteria Baglio della Luna

Via Serafino Amabile Guastella 1; tel: 0922 511 061; www.bagliodellaluna.com; €€€–€€€€

Set in the countryside, this traditional family-run Sicilian manor house (*baglio*) has been exquisitely restored and furnished with Sicilian antiques and paintings. Bedrooms are divided between the guesthouse and the ancient watchtower. The hotel features charming courtyards, a lush garden and solarium with jacuzzi. It also boasts a noted restaurant.

Tre Torri

Viale Cannatello 7; tel: 0922 606 733; www.hoteltretorri.eu; €€

This large 3-star hotel is conveniently situated, just east of the temples and at walking distance from the city centre. There is a restaurant, a bar, indoor and outdoor swimming pools, and a very pleasant sauna.

Villa Athena

Via Passeggiata Archeologica 33;

A suite at the Kempinski   *Villa Athena in the Valley of the Temples*

tel: 0922 596 288; www.hotelvillaathena.it; €€€€

Newly renovated and effortlessly romantic, this 18th-century villa has a wonderful setting amid gardens and olive trees in the Valley of the Temples. The five-star boutique hotel has comfortably furnished rooms, most with balconies overlooking the pool and Temple of Concordia. This is one of Sicily's most popular hotels, so be sure to book well in advance.

Piazza Armerina

Suite d'Autore

Piazza Duomo; tel: 0935 688 553; www.suitedautore.it; €€–€€€

Conceived as an art and design gallery, this bohemian boutique hotel will appeal to artists and urbanites. The provocative, art-studded rooms have titles such as Lightness or Magic and Irony; suites overlook the cathedral. Take breakfast in the rooftop bar overlooking the city.

Park Hotel Paradiso

Contrada Ramalda; tel: 0935 680 841; www.parkhotelparadiso.it; €€

This hotel boasts friendly owners and a convenient location for visiting the Villa Romana. It is cosy and sophisticated with a swimming pool and tennis courts, and the surrounding park is particularly pleasant.

Villa Trigona

Contrada Bauccio; tel: 0935 681 896; www.villatrigona.it; €–€€

The noble Trigona family's baronial country villa outside Piazza Armerina is now an engaging B&B packed with old-world charm. Don't miss the wonderful, good-value dinner (approx. €30), which uses locally sourced produce. There is also a newly added swimming pool.

Siracusa

B&B Dolce Casa

Loc. Fontane Bianche Via Lido Sacramento 4; tel: 0931 721 135; www.bbdolcecasa. it; €–€€.

With its tranquil garden and old-world charm, this noted villa B&B makes a charming base from which to enjoy the countryside, the beach and the historical sights. The villa is only 10 minutes from one of Siracusa's best beaches, Fontane Bianche. The other draw is the food, with tasty home-made pastries produced for breakfast.

Caol Ishka

Via Elorina, Contrada Pantanelli; tel: 0931 69057; www.caolishka.com; €€–€€€

Set 2km (1.25 miles) outside Siracusa, on the banks of the Anapo River, this arty boutique hotel is run by a Sicilian-Irish couple. With a swimming pool, stylish bar, friendly service and noted gastronomic restaurant, it offers a peaceful haven from the city.

Domus Mariae

Via Vittorio Veneto 76; tel: 0931 24854; www.domusmariaebenessere.com; €–€€

Reading room at Caol Ishka in Siracusa

Set in a restored ancient building in the historic centre, this small hotel with 12 rooms is run by nuns, who offer a warm welcome and good service.

Grand Hotel Ortigia
Viale Mazzini 12; tel: 0931 464 600; www.grandhotelortigia.it; €€€€
The best place to stay in Siracusa, this appealingly renovated Art Nouveau hotel overlooks Porto Grande and the yacht marina. The roof garden is home to an excellent Sicilian restaurant and enjoys panoramic views.

Gutowski
Lungomare Vittorini 26; tel: 0931 465 861; www.guthotel.it; €€
A small but comfortable hotel on the sea in Ortigia. There are 13 rooms and a small sunny terrace with panoramic views where they serve a delicious chocolate *granita*. Rich breakfast and friendly service, small dogs accepted.

Mercure Siracusa Prometeo
Viale Teracati 20; tel: 0931 464646; www.mercure.com; €€
Contemporary architecture meets the city's classic setting at this branch of the Mercure hotel chain, just steps away from the archaeological area. The 93 rooms are comfortable and well-equipped, and the pleasant swimming pool is perfect to cool off in the Sicilian summer. There is also a gym, and a wellness centre with a Turkish bath, Jacuzzis and massages. Babysitting available upon request.

Palazzo del Sale
Via Santa Teresa 25, Ortigia; tel: 0931 65958; www.palazzodelsale.com; €€
Set in a former salt workshop, this quirky but upmarket B&B is decorated in warm colours, and is convenient for exploring the most atmospheric part of Siracusa: the island of Ortigia.

Principe di Fitalia
Via Traversa Tonnara di Terrauzza 38; tel: 0931 485064; www.hotelprincipedifitalia. it; €€€
This luxurious hotel is housed in a large villa from the late 1800s set amongst well-kept palm and olive groves. The interior is traditional style with a twist, featuring antique furniture, wrought iron, old paintings and colourful local ceramics. Facilities include a large breakfast room with a view of the garden, a wellness centre and a beautiful swimming pool surrounded by a sandy beach.

Noto

Centro Storico
Corso Vittorio Emanuele 64; tel: 0931 812 063 and 0931 573 967; www.centro-storico.com; €
A quaint B&B in the centre of historic Noto, with en suite rooms. The décor is very simple and air conditioning is available. No credit cards accepted. Note that the hotel is closed Feb, Nov, and Dec.

Masseria degli Ulivi
Strada Statale 287; tel: 0931 813019; www.masseriadegliulivi.com; €€

A more traditional room   *Ornate Noto balcony*

Part of an old farm estate, this cottage complex located in the Noto countryside is the perfect spot for those looking to spend some quiet time in a beautiful bucolic setting. The bungalow-style rooms guarantee maximum privacy and are furnished with taste, and there is also a marvellous swimming pool. The restaurant serves local dishes.

Seven Rooms Villadorata

Via Nicolaci 18; tel: 338 509 5643; www.7roomsvilladorata.it; €€€€

Set in grandiose Palazzo Nicolaci, this smart B&B respects the 18th-century spirit of the palace. The seven rooms, all with balconies, overlook the cathedral, and are decorated with fine furnishings. Views from the terrace, where breakfast is served, are sublime.

Módica

Balarte Hotel

Contrada da Scorrione; tel: 0932 779 014; www.balartehotel.it; €€

Set in an old *masseria* (farmhouse) outside town, this arty hotel makes an appealing prospect, with delicious local food served for breakfast, including crêpes made with carob flour and stuffed with ricotta and chocolate.

Ferro Hotel

Via Stazione SN; tel: 0932 941 043; www.ferrohotel.it; €€

This quirky station hotel is at the very end of the Módica station platform, even if trains are rare so sleep is guaranteed.

The whole hotel evokes the train theme, including the restaurant, Binario 4 (Platform 4).

Il Cavaliere

Corso Umberto I, 259; tel: 0932 947 219; www.palazzoilcavaliere.it; €

On the main street of Módica, this is a lovely B&B with friendly owners set in an elegant early 19th-century palazzo. Rooms are individually furnished and retain original features such as frescoes and exposed stonework.

Palazzo Failla

Via Blandini 5; tel: 0932 941 059; www.palazzofailla.it; €€–€€€

This beguiling boutique hotel in Módica Alta is suffused with Sicilian charm – left much as it was when the owners lived there, but brought bang up to date with the addition of a Michelin-starred chef. There are gorgeous rooms in the main building with frescoed ceilings and chandeliers, with more modern ones in the annexe.

Pietre Nere Resort

Pietre Nere, Via Pietre Nere Cava Ispica 142; 0932 753051; www.pietrenereresort.it; €€€

This resort features 28 rooms overlooking the Módica countryside, and is located less than 1 km away from the archaeological area of Ispica. Rooms are modern and classy, with a prevalence of white and black, and the large breakfast also offers options for gluten-

Balcony view from the San Domenico Palace, Taormina

intolerant guests. There is also a swimming pool.

Ragusa

Artemisia Resort
Via E. Caruso 13; tel: 0932 642 575; www.artemisiaresort.com; €€

In the countryside on the outskirts of Ragusa, this lovely boutique hotel is cared for by gracious owners who also run a noted *pasticceria*, hence delicious Mòdica-style pastries for breakfast. Hang by the pool, explore the Montalbano Detective Trail (ask for a map) or head to the nearby beach.

Locanda Don Serafino
Via XI Febbraio 15, Ragusa Ibla; tel: 0932 222 0065; www.locandadonserafino.it; €€–€€€

This inviting boutique hotel, excavated from the rock face, houses 10 elegant guest rooms. The renowned restaurant, with a Michelin star, is 10 minutes' walk away (see page 116).

Risveglio Ibleo
Largo Camerina 3, Ragusa Ibla; tel: 0932 247 811; www.risveglioibleo.com; €

This 19th-century palazzo has been converted into a B&B with four self-catering rooms in the main house and two less stylish ones at the back. The owner takes pride in serving breakfast in his own dining room: Arab biscuits, thyme-flavoured *dolce*, fresh ricotta and bread with home-made marmalade and Ragusa honey.

Chiaramonte Gulfi

Antica Stazione
Via Madonna Santissimo Rosario, SP n. 8, Km 3; tel: 0932 928 083; www.anticastazione.com; €

Set in the Iblei mountains, this hugely friendly, family-run hotel was once a railway station. Although convenient for both Ragusa and Chiaramonte, the hotel feels peacefully aloof, set among carob trees. Warm, professional service is complemented by quiet rooms, a very popular restaurant and low prices.

Valle di Chiaramonte
Contrada Piano Zacchi - Pantanelli; tel: 0932 926 079; www.valledichiaramonte. it; €

This friendly *agriturismo* is made up of clusters of rustic self-catering apartments. Guests can enjoy the farm-grown produce, from aromatic olive oil to salami, cooked meats and mature Ragusano DOP cheese.

Catania

5 Balconi B&B
Via Plebiscito 133; tel: 0957 234 534; www.5balconi.it; €

On the second floor of a palazzo (with lift) and close to the castle, this welcoming B&B has three cosy guest rooms, one with a volcano view. The rooms share a bathroom and shower room. Rob (English) and Cristina (Sicilian) are hugely helpful hosts and will tell you all about the region over the delicious breakfast. No credit cards accepted.

San Domenico Palace suite   *View of Etna from Taormina's Grand Hotel Timeo*

Donna Carmela
Contrada Grotte 5, Carruba di Riposto; tel: 095 809 383; www.donnacarmela.com; €€–€€€

This charming hotel is set in a historic villa built in the 1800s, but has very modern interiors. The owners cultivate flowers for sale, and offer guided tours to their Mediterranean flora greenhouses and fields. Good restaurant with a menu based on local specialities from the Catania area.

EH13 B&B
Via Sant'Euplio 13; tel: 095 715 2216; www.eh13.it; €€

This boutique bed-and-breakfast is furnished with a mix of designer furniture, ethnic objects, Baroque-inspired pieces and high-quality technological accessories. Conveniently located in the heart of Catania's historic centre, this hotel also offers magnificent views of Mount Etna. Breakfast is traditional Sicilian featuring organic local ingredients.

Etnea 316
Via Etnea 316; tel: 0952 503 076; www.hoteletnea316.it; €

A refurbished B&B that offers a lovely home-away-from-home feeling, with spacious, beautifully decorated rooms and a welcoming atmosphere.

UNA Hotel Palace
Via Etnea 218; tel: 095 250 5111; www.unahotels.it; €€–€€€

Part of the UNA chain, this is a luxury hotel on the main shopping street. The 94 rooms' decor is minimalist with bold colours. Locals flock to the roof garden bar for *aperitivi* with views of Etna.

Taormina

Grand Hotel Miramare
Via Guardiola Vecchia 27; tel: 0942 23401; www.miramaretaormina.it; €€€€

This welcoming hotel is housed in an elegant building. There are 68 rooms with Wi-Fi, swimming pool, parking, tennis, gardens and splendid sea views. The hotel is closed mid-Nov–mid-Dec.

Grand Hotel Timeo
Via Teatro Greco 59; tel: 0942 627 0200; www.grandhoteltimeo.com; €€€€

Set beside the Teatro Greco, Sicily's grandest hotel is impeccably run by the Orient Express group and has been restored to its original splendour. Airy, sophisticated suites have wonderful views over terraced gardens and the sea. A shuttle runs to the private beach at its sister hotel in summer. It also boasts an outstanding gastronomic restaurant (see page 84).

San Domenico Palace
Piazza San Domenico 5; tel: 0942 613 111; www.san-domenico-palace.com; €€€€

Perfect for romantic history-lovers, this former Dominican monastery feels like a living museum and a private world,

Hammock with a view of Strómboli, Panarea

with several cloisters, gorgeous gardens and more public rooms than any other hotel. The top suite has a jacuzzi on the terrace. Some rooms are grand, others are smaller, though all are atmospheric. Views are magnificent, especially from the terrace towards Etna and the sea. Cuisine is also outstanding, with two Michelin-starred restaurants.

Villa Belvedere
Via Bagnoli Croce 79; tel: 0942 23791; www.villabelvedere.it; €€€

This inviting villa hotel with stunning views sits on a hillside just above the botanical gardens, with semi-tropical grounds surrounding a lavish swimming pool. Every room has a balcony or terrace – those in the villa, the older section of the hotel, are especially atmospheric with intricate terracotta flooring and antique furnishings aplenty.

Villa Diodoro
Via Bagnoli Croci 75; tel: 0942 23312; www.gaishotels.com; €€€€

Only a few minutes' stroll into the centre, this hotel is popular for both its pool and restaurant, which have wonderful panoramic views of Mount Etna and the coastline. Guests also have access to the sister hotel's private beach.

Villa Greta
Via Leonardo da Vinci 46; tel: 0942 28286; www.villagreta.it; €€

A small, family-run hotel which is surprisingly affordable, considering most rooms come with a balcony and incredible views. It's a 15-minute walk from Taormina on the Castelmola road and about 800 m from the cable car.

Villa Fiorita
Via Pirandello 39; tel: 0942 24122; www.villafioritahotel.com; €€

This lovely hotel is located on the hillside edging the town. There are 25 pleasant rooms, many with wonderful views overlooking the Mediterranean. Lush garden and a terrace with lounge chairs.

Villa Schuler
Piazzetta Bastione 16; tel: 0942 23481; www.hotelvillaschuler.com; €€

This villa hotel, which has been in the same family since 1905, serves up elegant old-world charm and splendid views of Etna and the Bay of Naxos. Rooms overlook the large subtropical garden or out to sea (rates vary accordingly). A minimum two-night stay is required during high season. Free bikes are available for guests.

Villa Taormina
Via Fazzello 49; Tel: 0942 620 072; www.hotelvillataormina.com; €€€€

A charming boutique hotel, with rooms full of antiques in the traditional style of a Sicilian luxury home. The hotel also has a lovely terrace with magnificent view of the sea and the hills,

Rustic accommodation

parking and a shuttle service to the beach.

Aeolian Islands

Diana Brown
Vico Himera 3, Lípari; tel: 090 981 2584; www.dianabrown.it; €
Run by a friendly South African-Sicilian couple, this B&B five minutes' walk from the port has 12 refurbished rooms (five with self-catering facilities) and a lovely roof terrace.

Gattopardo Park
Viale Diana, Lipari; tel: 0909 811 035; www.gattopardoparkhotel.it; €€€
Located near the centre of Lípari, this 18th-century villa offers a marvellous swimming pool and private bungalows. Open Mar–Oct.

Giardino sul Mare
Via Maddalena 65, Lipari; tel: 0909 811 004; www.giardinosulmare.it; €-€€
This small hotel is on the sea and not far from the centre of Lípari. The views are great, breakfast is reasonable, and there is also a pleasant swimming pool and a direct access to sea.

Hotel Rocce Azzurre
Via Maddalena 69, Lípari; tel: 090 9813 248; www.hotelrocce azzurre.it; €-€€
This hotel on the water's edge has restful, refurbished rooms and gorgeous sea views. The bathing platform with sunbeds is perfect for chilling out. Half board only in peak season.

Lisca Bianca
Via Lani 1, Panarea; tel: 090 983004; www.liscabianca.it; €€€
Situated right in front of the tourist harbour, this hotel has 25 rooms (each with a balcony), a beach and a swimming pool. The grounds are large and lush. Open Apr–end-Oct.

Raya
Via San Pietro, Panarea; tel: 090 983 013; www.hotelraya.it; €€€€
This landmark hotel is at once contemporary and timeless, set on the most chic island in the Aeolians yet still laidback and effortlessly charming. A favourite among celebrities.

Capofaro Malvasia & Resort
Via Faro 3, Salina; tel: 090 984 4330; www.capofaro.it; €€€-€€€€
This feels like essence of Mediterranean in its 'barefoot luxury' simplicity, matched by sea views, Malvasia vineyards, spa treatments and whitewashed interiors on the island where *Il Postino* was filmed.

Signum
Via Scalo 15, Malfa, Salina; tel: 0909 844 222; www.hotelsignum.it; €€€€
This luxury boutique hotel boasts sea and garden views, fragrant lemon and jasmine trees, and whitewashed interiors. With an infinity pool and whirlpool, natural hot springs, shady verandahs and fine dining by the sea, you'll find it hard to tear yourself away.

RESTAURANTS

Sicily's ancient, distinguished cuisine is among the most pleasurable discoveries you'll make on the island. Sicilian chefs used to be snapped up by starry establishments abroad, but many of today's culinary talents are now showcasing their skills at home. Along with the grand gastronomic restaurants, there are wonderful street snacks – especially in the markets, where some stalls will grill fish, squid and octopus while you wait. And between the two, you'll find plenty of *trattorie* serving authentic Sicilian dishes.

The southeast of the island, especially Ragusa, Módica and Chiaramonte Gulfi, is the current culinary hotspot, with some of the most varied and creative cooking in Sicily. Palermo and Catania both have excellent and diverse restaurants, and sophisticated Taormina has an array of gastronomic tables. Prices here are higher than anywhere else on the island.

Lunch is usually served from 1pm to 3pm and dinner from 8pm to 10.30pm or later. Nearly all restaurants display a menu outside with prices. Beware of the fixed-price menus in tourist resorts, which are often poor value, and instead try to pick restaurants which are frequented by locals. Most restaurant bills include a service charge (usually 10 percent) and many add a *coperto* (cover charge) as well, from €1 to €4 per person. See also Food and Drink, page 14, and the food and drink boxes throughout the Best Routes section.

Price for a two-course meal for one person, including a glass of wine and service:
€€€€ = over €40
€€€ = €30–40
€€ = €20–30
€ = under €20

Palermo

Al Covo dei Beati Paoli
Piazza Marina 50; tel: 091 616 6634; www.alcovodeibeatipaoli.com; daily; €€
With tables set out on Palermo's prettiest piazza, this is a pleasant spot in summer. In winter, guests can enjoy the medieval-inspired interior. Appetisers include *caponata* and lamb skewers, and the baked suckling kid is delicious. The pizzas are good, but service can be slow.

Antico Caffè Spinnato
Via Principe di Belmonte 115; tel: 091 329 220; daily 7am–1am; €
Located in a chic, central pedestrianised zone, this is where the smart set come for *aperitivi*. The Spinnato group is known for its superb ice creams, *cassata* and *Cannoli*, served here and at Al Pinguino (Via Ruggiero Settimo 86) and Il

Cannoli, a Sicilian speciality

Golosone (Piazza Castelnuovo 22). Pastas, grills and salads are also available.

Cucina Papoff
Via Isidoro la Lumia 32; tel: 091 586 460; D Mon–Sat, closed Aug; www.cucina papoff.com; €€€

This welcoming little *trattoria* near Teatro Massimo serves imaginative Sicilian cuisine in the vaults of an 18th-century building. Try *frittella* (artichokes, fava beans and peas), followed by swordfish in a caper sauce. On a chilly day, order *u maccu*, a creamy soup of fava beans with wild fennel.

Gigi Mangia
Via Principe di Belmonte 104; tel: 091 587 651; L and D Mon–Sat; €€

Set on an elegant pedestrianised street, this is a *trattoria* with a delicatessen attached that delivers food and wine worldwide. Menu highlights include a selection of delicious vegetarian appetisers and *colonnello piero va a favignana* – a pasta dish with tomatoes, herbs and *bottarga* (tuna roe).

Osteria dei Vespri
Piazza Croce dei Vespri 6; tel: 091 617 1631; www.osteriadeivespri.it; L and D Mon–Sat; €€€

This old tavern occupies the former coach house of 18th-century Palazzo Gangi. It's set on a lovely sheltered square with tables outdoors in summer. The cooking is creative Italian, with artfully presented dishes. Try ravioli stuffed with baked ricotta, fried courgettes and lemon served with *bottarga* (dried and salted tuna roe), followed by fresh fish or meat (suckling pig, quail or beef). The wine list has more than 350 labels to choose from.

Santandrea
Piazza Sant'Andrea 4; tel: 091 334 999; D only Mon–Sat; www.ristorante santandrea.eu; €€€

Set a stone's throw from the Vucciria Market, this gourmet trattoria is perfect for an alfresco dinner. Try the seafood antipasti feast and the pasta dishes, notably the *pappardelle* pasta with capon, artichokes and wild fennel.

Tonnara Bordonaro
Via Bordonaro 9; tel: 091 637 2267; www.kursaaltonnara.it; Mon–Sat L and D, Sun L; €€

Set in a converted tuna fishery in Arenella, on the edge of town, this is an inviting spot in summer, with a boat-shaped bar in the courtyard and a restaurant that embraces a lovely terrace and sea views. Try the risotto, tuna or swordfish carpaccio. Live music.

Mondello

Bye Bye Blues
Via del Garofalo 23; tel: 091 684 1415; L and D Tue–Sat, closed Nov; www.byebyeblues.it; €€€

Don't be put off by the nightclub name – this gastronomic restaurant on the road into Mondello is superb. A minimalist

Tables set for dinner, Cefalù

dining room (simple black chairs, plain white walls) is the setting for Patrizia di Benedetto's Michelin-starred Mediterranean cuisine, presented with plenty of flair. Typical dishes include prawn carpaccio and squid salad, Sicilian cheese soufflé or black lasagne with codfish and pumpkin purée.

Charleston le Terrazze

Via Regina Elena; tel: 091 450 171; www.alleterrazze.it; L and D, Closed Wed Nov–Apr and early Jan–early Feb €€€€

Set in an Art Nouveau beach establishment, this gracious spot is particularly good for fish. The chef pays particular attention to ingredient selection, and even the bread is baked in-house. Well-stocked wine cellar and impeccable service. Book ahead.

Cefalù

Lo Scoglio Ubriaco

Via Carlo Ortolani di Bordonaro 2; tel: 0921 423 228; L and D daily (closed Tue in winter and 6 Jan–6 Feb); €–€€

The handsome terrace here overlooks the harbour, so you can watch the fishing boats while enjoying *spaghetti al cartoccio di mare* (spaghetti with seafood, sealed in a bag and baked), plus grilled or fried fish. Pizzas are served in the evenings.

Kentia al Trappitu

Via Calo Ortolani di Bordonaro 96; tel: 0921 423 801; L and D Wed–Mon, closed Jan; €€€

Known for its charm, cuisine and lovely terrace overlooking the sea. The fish arrives daily and the meat menu is rich and interesting. Sample the *scaloppine ai funghi* (mushroom and veal escalope) and *panzerotti di magro* (fried ravioli filled with ricotta and spinach).

Monreale

Bricco & Bacco

Via B. D'Aquisito 13, Monreale; tel: 091 641 7773; L and D daily except Sun Jun–Aug, except Mon in winter; €€€

This is a haven for carnivores with a great mixed grill. There is no fish or pasta – but excellent antipasti and mouthwatering desserts. Other plus points are a warm, friendly atmosphere, attentive service and good wines to complement the meat.

Castelbuono

Nangalarruni

Via della Confraternite 5; tel: 0921 671228; www.hostariananangalarruni.it; L and D daily (closed Wed in winter); €€

Well-known chef Giuseppe Carollo showcases the best ingredients from the Madonie mountains, using everything from mushrooms to suckling pig and sheep's cheese. Wash it down with wine from the Santa Anastasia estate in the hills below town.

Alcamo

La Batia

Via Porta Palermo 106, Contrada Turchi; tel: 0924 25554; Tue–Sun 12.20–3pm, 7pm–

Swordfish hors d'œuvre

midnight; www.la-batia.it; €€

Set in an atmospheric former convent on the outskirts of Alcamo, this exceptional, great-value restaurant combines ambience and engaging service with authentic, sure-footed Sicilian cuisine. Subtle antipasti are followed by excellent meat and fish mains, as well as pizza, with *cannoli* for dessert. There's a good wine list too.

Sirignano Wine Resort

Contrada Sirignano; tel: 091 251 5281; www.sirignanowineresort.it; L daily (D on request); €€

Set among rolling vineyards 12km (7.5 miles) from Alcamo, this appealing wine resort is home to a remarkable chef who creates wonderful interpretations of classic Sicilian dishes with a delicate touch. Combine lunch with a wine tasting and tour around the organic winery, or even fall into one of the cosy beds. Lunch and visits with reservation only (meals are mainly lunch, but dinner is possible on request).

Trápani

Caupona Taverna di Sicilia

Piazza Purgatorio 32; tel: 0923 546 618; L and D Wed–Mon, open on Tue for D only from May to Oct, closed Feb; €€

The seafood here is superb: try the *caponata di pesce* (fish with aubergine, celery and capers in a sweet-and-sour sauce), *polpette al nero di sepia* (cuttlefish balls) or fish couscous. There's an excellent wine list too.

Taverna Paradiso

Lungomare D. Alighieri 22; tel: 0923 22303; L and D Mon–Sat; €€€.

A highly regarded inn right on the seafront, specialising in *neonata, spaghetti ai ricci* (spaghetti with sea urchins), octopus salad and tuna. Lovely outdoor patio on the beach. It is advisable to book ahead.

Erice

La Pentolaccia

Via G.F. Guarnotti 17; tel: 0923 869 099; www.ristorantelapentolaccia.it; L and D Wed–Mon, closed 6 Jan–6 Feb; €–€€

This restaurant in the centre of Erice occupies an old monastery. Dishes are all local, including some wonderful fish and couscous specials. Good choice of local wines.

Moderno

Via Vittorio Emanuele 67; tel: 0923 869 300; www.hotelmodernoerice.it; closed Mon in quiet season; €€€.

This charming family-run hotel restaurant serves classic Sicilian dishes including a delicious *caponata*. The décor is both elegant and sober and there is a beautiful terrace with panoramic views of the surrounding hills.

Monte San Giuliano

Vicolo San Rocco, 7, Erice; tel: 0923 869 595; www.montesangiuliano.it; L and D Tue–Sun; €€

This rustic-style inn boasts a delightful terraced garden and tasty traditional

La Madia in Licata, with two Michelin stars

Trapanese cooking. On the menu you'll find *involtini di melanzana* (stuffed aubergine rolls), pasta with Trapanese pesto, fresh shrimp and artichokes, or various grilled meats.

Mazara del Vallo

Alla Kasbah

Via Itria 10, Mazara del Vallo; tel: 0923 906 126; L and D Tue–Sun; €€

Set in the heart of town, and popular with the locals, this is a good place for fish couscous, *busiate* (pasta) with prawns and a mixed antipasto combining all the flavours of Sicily.

Marinella di Selinunte

Africa da Bruno

Via Alceste 24, Marinella di Selinunte; tel: 0924 46456; closed winter and Thur except Aug; €

This is a simple eatery with no sea views but instead excellent-value antipasti, pasta, fish and, in the evenings, a selection of pizzas *al legno* (in a wood-burning oven).

Pierrot

Via Pigafetta 108, Marinella di Selinunte; tel: 092 446 205; L and D daily Apr–Oct, L only Nov–Mar, closed early Jan to early Feb; €–€€

Come for fabulous sea views, fish of the day and pizzas. Specialities are *trenette ai ricci* (pasta with sea urchins), *spaghetti ai gamberi con asparagi e rucola* (with prawns, asparagus and rocket) and chargrilled fish.

Agrigento

Bar Ristorante La Promenade

Via Passeggiata Archeologica 12–14; tel: 0922 23715; Daily L and D; €

Situated between the temples and the town, the café and *pasticceria* are known for their almond treats: tuck into cakes, marzipan treats, *granite*, ice cream and *latte di mandorla* (a milky almond drink), while the restaurant serves fish and meat dishes. Lovely terraces in the front and in the back.

Trattoria Concordia

Via Porcello 8; tel: 0922 22668; L and D Mon–Sat. Closed Sun in winter; €€.

Good for grilled fish and seafood-based pasta dishes – try the spaghetti with prawns, or those with swordfish, eggplant and mint. The house wine is good. There are also reasonably priced fixed menus and outdoor seating in the summer.

Licata

La Madia

Corso Filippo Re Capriata 22; 0922 771 443; www.ristorantelamadia.it; L and D Mon, Wed–Sat, Sun L; €€€€

Licata is an ugly town marooned between Ragusa and Agrigento, but it boasts the island's most celebrated restaurant. Chef Pino Cuttaia delights with his inventive, two Michelin-starred cuisine. Typical is his version of *arancino* (a fried rice ball and classic Sicilian street snack) in a sauce of red mullet and wild fennel.

Anchovies in sea water

La Madia's chef Pino Cuttaia

Piazza Armerina

La Ruota

Contrada Paratore (near Villa Romana); tel: 0935 680 542; www.trattorialaruota.it; L daily; €€

Housed in a converted watermill, this attractive *trattoria* specialises in home-made pasta. Try the delicious *maccheroni*, fresh tomato pasta and *melanzane in agrodolce* (aubergines in sweet-and-sour vinaigrette), followed by roast pork or rabbit. The fresh ricotta and *primosale* pecorino cheeses are delicious with a glass of Nero d'Avola or Cerasuola di Vittoria. Booking is advisable.

Da Totò

Via Mazzini 29, Piazza Armerina; tel: 0935 680 153; L and D daily, closed Mon in winter; €

A popular spot with the locals who come for crispy pizzas, Chef Toto's handmade *pappardelle* (pasta) or *bocca di lupo*, steak with prosciutto, mozzarella and aubergine.

Siracusa

Dioniso

Via Claudio Maria Arezzo 29, Ortigia; tel: 0931 124679; €€

The atmosphere is somewhat classy at this upscale trattoria. The menu lists a good selection of fish specialties including the popular tuna steak, but also Sicilian favourites such as *melanzane alla parmigiana*. Portions are not big but quality is high.

Don Camillo

Via Maestranza 96; tel: 0931 67133; www.ristorantedoncamillosiracusa.it; L and D Mon–Sat Closed second and third week of Jan and Jul; €€€

An old Ortigia favourite, this well-known restaurant near the centre serves some wonderful variations on local specialities, including pasta with cuttlefish in its own ink, *zuppa di mucco* (fish soup) or grilled tuna steak. The well-stocked cellar has a choice of 700 wines, with emphasis on Sicily. Reservations are recommended.

La Foglia

Via Capodieci 29, Ortigia; tel: 0931 66 233; www.lafoglia.it; L and D Wed–Mon; €€

Renowned more for its quirky decor and atmosphere than its cuisine, the restaurant is owned by a sculptor and is packed with paintings, statuary and mixed crockery. A limited menu offers soups, vegetarian platters and seafood dishes.

Taverna Giudecca Ortigia

Via della Giudecca 7, Ortigia; tel: 329 635 6563; €

This small but welcoming trattoria specialises in what is known as *aperi-cena*, a dinner made of tapa-like local specialties ranging from cured meats, cheese platters, baked ricotta and experimental recipes made with local ingredients. Great selection of Sicilian wines.

Waiting for customers

Noto

Il Barocco

Ronco Sgadari 8; tel: 0931 835 999; €€

This small restaurant has an atmospheric courtyard setting and serves traditional dishes – pasta, pizza, grilled meat and fish, cooked with simple ingredients.

Pasticceria Kennedy

Via Principe Umberto 128; €

Noto's most popular bakery and pastry shop. Choose among *cannoli*, *cassate*, ricotta cheese cakes, candied fruits, chocolate, and much more. There is also a good selection of savoury snacks for the perfect lunch picnic.

Trattoria del Carmine

Via Ducezio 9; tel: 0931 838 705; www.trattoriadelcarmine.it; Tue–Sun 11am–10pm; €

Everything at this simple, family-run trattoria is fresh and home-made. Regional specialities include seafood-based pastas and *coniglio alla stimpirate*, a traditional Sicilian rabbit dish with a sweet-and-sour sauce. Pizzas are also served in the evening.

Ragusa

Baglio la Pergola

Piazza Luigi Sturzo, Contrada Selvaggio; tel: 0932 686 43; www.baglio.it; L and D Wed–Mon, closed in Aug; €€€

Popular, elegant spot for updated versions of local dishes. Sample ricotta ravioli with a *ragú* of suckling pig, or the *maccheroncini* with the pistachio pesto. Second courses are mainly meaty, but some fish is listed on the menu too.

Locandina Don Serafino

Via Avvocato Ottaviano 13, Ragusa Ibla; tel: 0932 248 778; www.locandadon serafino.it; L and D Wed–Mon; €€€–€€€€

Burrowed into the basement of an atmospheric mansion, this is one of Sicily's most seductive restaurants. The delectable cuisine ranges from seafood salad to sophisticated interpretations of Sicilian street food (rice balls with saffron) or Ragusan rabbit. The boutique hotel is equally lovely (see page 106).

Monna Lisa

Via Ettore Fieramosca; tel: 0932 642 250; www.monnalisaragusa.com; L and D Tue–Sun; €€

Richly flavoured Sicilian dishes in large trattoria with a garden. Try the pasta with eggplant and swordfish, or one of the many risotti. Pizza in evenings. Fixed-price lunch menu for €10.

La Piazzetta

Piazza Duomo 14; tel: 0932 686 131; www.lapiazzettaragusaibla.it; daily L and D; €€

Genuine *cucina ragusana* so grilled vegetables, *impanate* (Sicilian pasty), *cavatelli ragusani*, cheeses and an array of meats, but little fish. Wide selection of Sicilian and Italian wines including great Passitos.

Sicilian Christmas pastries　　　　　　　　*Al fresco lunch in Taormina*

Chiaramonte Gulfi

Antica Stazione

Contrada Santissimo; tel: 0932 928 083; L and D Tue–Sun; €

Set in an old railway station, this easygoing trattoria and pizzeria (with a summer terrace) is popular with locals. Dishes use delicious Chiaramonte olive oil and Ragusan cheeses. The meat and fish set menus are both superb value.

Catania

La Cantinaccia

Via Calatafimi 1/a; tel: 095 537 291; Tue–Sun L and D, closed in Aug; €€

This upmarket but intimate restaurant is designed in rustic style. The cuisine is international and Sicilian with pizza served in the evening. They also have a good selection of artisanal beers.

La Marchesana

Via Mazza 4; tel: 095 315 171; www.lamarchesana.com; L and D; €€

The menu is particularly strong on fish at this small restaurant, and the friendly owners offer a warm welcome. Eat outside in fine weather, or inside in the elegant vaulted dining room.

Menza

Viale Mario Rapisardi 143; tel: 095 350 606; www.menza.it; Mon–Sun all day; €–€€

This is a typical Sicilian *rosticceria* with takeaway roast meats and street snacks: try the *arancini* (savoury filled rice balls), sweet *crespelle* (pancakes) with honey or the delicious pastries.

Osteria I Tre Bicchieri

Via San Giuseppe al Duomo 31; tel: 095 715 3540; www.osteriaitrebicchieri.it; D Mon–Sat; €€€–€€€€

Northwest of the cathedral, behind the university, this sophisticated spot offers the best dining experience in Catania. Head to the vaulted dining room to sample creative and beautifully presented Mediterranean cuisine, with wonderful seafood pasta and local fish, or the Cantina wine bar in the same building for cheaper international dishes.

La Siciliana

Viale Marco Polo 52; tel: 095 376 400; www.lasiciliana.it; L and D Tue–Sat, L Sun; €€€

Set within a 19th-century villa in a charming garden setting, La Siciliana is quite a way north of the centre (and expensive by local standards), but it's well worth the trip. Specialities include roast lamb, carpaccio of fresh swordfish and imaginative vegetable dishes, served with excellent local wines. There is a smoking section. Reservations are essential.

Trattoria Il Mare

Via S. Michele, 7; tel: 095 317024; www.trattoriailmare.com; L and D Tues-Sun; €–€€

Just off the main tourist drag this family-run, simply-furnished trattoria has first-class seafood. The fish antipasti is a real feast.

Taormina

L'Arco dei Cappuccini
Via Cappuccini, 1, near Porta Messina;
tel: 0942 24893; L and D Thu–Tue;
€€€
This busy, welcoming restaurant is where
the smart set gather. The excellent Sicilian cooking has an emphasis on fresh
fish as well as meat. The selection of
Sicilian wines and liqueurs is good too.
Reservations recommended.

Bar Turrisi
Via Pio IX, 16, Castelmola; tel: 0942 28181;
daily all day; €
This eccentric bar in the village of Castelmola, 5km (3 miles) above Taormina, has
fine rooftop views of the Etna, a decent
pasta and pizza menu, and a large collection of Sicilian memorabilia, including
conspicuous phallic figurines. Almond
wine, 'the elixir of love', is the speciality
of the house.

Bella Blu
Via Luigi Pirandello 28; tel: 0942 24239;
www.bellablutaormina.com; L and D daily;
€–€€
This buzzing restaurant, pizzeria, piano
bar and disco is an entertaining and
chic place to spend an evening. Menu
highlights include grills and barbecued
meats, plus pasta with sardines. Reserve
ahead in summer.

La Capinera
Via Nazionale 177; tel: 338 158 8013; Tue–
Sun L and D; €€–€€€

This Michelin-starred haunt favours
local, seasonal produce from all over Sicily. From the home-made breads to the
fish dishes, this is an excellent choice.

La Giara
Vico la Floresta 1; tel: 0942 23360;
www.lagiara-taormina.com; Closed Mon
and Nov, Feb, Mar; €€€€
This respected restaurant and piano bar
is also a popular nightlife destination
among chic locals. The dining experience is an elegant one, on roof or terraces with traditional menu and service.
Dress smart. Advance booking strongly
recommended.

Granduca
Corso Umberto I, 172; tel: 0942 24983;
www.granduca-taormina.com; L and D
Mon–Sat. Closed on Tue in winter;
€€€€
This charmingly cluttered restaurant,
filled with antiques, offers lovely views
over the bay. The price is for the view as
much as the food. The regional menu
offers home-made pastas topped with
rich sauces of aubergine, capers and
tuna, along with fresh fish dishes such
as *involtini di spade alla griglia* – grilled
swordfish rolls stuffed with breadcrumbs and parsley.

Mamma Rosa
Via Naumachie 10; tel: 0942 24361;
www.mammarosataormina.com; closed Tue
in winter; €€€
With tables lining the lively alley in the

The dining room at Principe di Cerami in Taormina

summer months, this busy spot serves up crispy pizzas, cooked in a wood-fired oven, as well as standard Italian fare.

Principe di Cerami
Hotel San Domenico Palace, Piazza San Domenico 5; tel: 0942 613 111; D Tue–Sun, closed Nov–Mar; €€€€

This elegant gourmet restaurant, with two Michelin stars to its name, is set in the gorgeous San Domenico hotel, which was formerly a monastery. Dine on the terrace in summer.

Pizzeria Vecchia Taormina
Vico Ebrei 3; tel: 0942 625 589; L and D Thu–Tue, D only July–Aug; €

An excellent pizzeria in the heart of town, with a wood-burning oven and courtyard seating.

Capri Leone (Messina)

Antica Filanda
Contrada Raviola; tel: 0941 919 704; L and D Tue–Sun, closed mid-Jan–mid-Feb; www.anticafilanda.net; €€

Overlooking the Aeolian Islands, this restaurant focuses on produce and dishes from the Nebrodi mountains. Expect the likes of black Nebrodi pork, Montalbano provola cheese, ricotta and Nebrodi goat's cheese.

Aeolian Islands

Capofaro
Via Faro 3, Salina; tel: 091 984 4330; www.capofaro.it; L and D Tue–Sun, closed May, mid-Oct–mid-Apr; €€€€

This romantic Michelin-starred restaurant in a luxury hotel draws a chic, moneyed crowd. The setting is elegant but relaxed, with a lovely terrace by the pool. If you're inspired by the cuisine (highly likely), consider booking one of the cookery classes.

Cincotta
Via San Pietro; tel: 090 983 014; www.hotelcincotta.it; Daily Apr–Oct; €€€€

Smart hotel with smart restaurant, where people dress down expensively and eat costly fish. The views are wonderful and the cuisine based on fish, with the freshest ingredients.

Hycesia
Via San Pietro; tel: 090 983 041; www.hycesia.it; Open daily, closed Nov–Mar; €€€

Named after the old word for Panarea, this chic spot near the port offers sophisticated, inventive cuisine, but still based on the catch of the day. Popular with the smart set. Great wine list.

Kasbah
Via Maurolico 25, Lípari; tel: 090 981 1075; D Thur–Tue (daily June–Sept), closed Nov–Mar; €€

This fashionable eatery has a contemporary white dining area and a charming candlelit garden with orange trees and roses. It's popular for its outstanding pizzas, but also offers a tempting menu featuring authentic Sicilian fish dishes.

NIGHTLIFE

Sicily may not be renowned for its night-clubs and discos, but Palermo, Catania and Siracusa offer a vibrant cultural scene, and there's no shortage of late-night bars in the main towns and coastal resorts. Taormina boasts the most sophisticated and expensive nightlife, ranging from summer dance clubs and live events at the Greek Theatre to ape-ritifs at elegant Etna-view bars or an evening *passeggiata* along the main street. Palermo pretty much empties out on summer evenings, when locals decamp to the fashionable beach resort of Mondello. Catania is the coolest and liveliest city for nightlife, with plenty of late-night bars and music venues.

Some of the most memorable perfor-mances – Greek plays, concerts, ballet, dance, jazz – are linked to the sum-mer festivals, held from June to August. Check with local tourist boards for a list of events or look in the two main news-papers, *Il Giornale di Sicilia* and *La Sicilia*.

The following listings include cultural venues, plus a small selection of lively nightclubs and bars.

Palermo

Teatro Massimo
Piazza Verdi; tel: 091 605 3521; www.teatromassimo.it; guided tours Tue–Sun 9.30am–4.30pm
The opera house offers a wonderful pro-gramme of ballet and opera. Dominating Piazza Verdi, it's the largest opera house in Italy, and the third-largest in Europe. The last scenes of *The Godfather Part III* were filmed here. The opera season runs from late September to late June.

Teatro Politeama Garibaldi
Piazza Ruggero Settimo; tel: 091 605 3421; www.orchestrasinfonicasiciliana.eu
This neoclassical-style theatre stages classical concerts and ballet, plus occa-sional jazz and contemporary music. It's currently closed for restoration.

Lo Spasimo
Via dello Spasimo; tel: 091 843 1605
This atmospheric entertainment com-plex is set in a former 16th-century mon-astery and was one of the first projects during the regeneration of the La Kalsa quarter. Classical and jazz concerts are held in the cloisters and the roofless church – on a sultry, starry night, with the swaying palms in the background, the atmosphere is wonderfully roman-tic. Some of the events are free.

Antico Caffè Spinnato
Via Principe di Belmonte 107; tel: 091 329 220; www.spinnato.it
Via Principe di Belmonte is a chic, cen-tral pedestrianised zone where the smart set gather at alfresco bars for *aperitivi*. The elegant Antico Caffè Spin-nato is the best-known venue, with a

Teatro Massimo in Palermo

reputation for superb ice creams, *cassata* and *cannoli*. It's also a great people-watching spot.

Kursaal Kalhesa

Foro Italico 21; tel: 091 616 2282; www.kursaalkalhesa.it
This eclectic café, restaurant, arty wine bar, concert venue and mellow club is set within La Kalsa's ancient stone walls. Evenings with live music draw a large local crowd.

Taormina

Morgana Bar

Scesa Morgana; tel: 094 262 0056; www.morganataormina.it
This late-night cocktail bar, decorated in timewarp 1960s Surrealist style, has a tiny dancefloor and decent cocktails. Don't expect the action really to get going until midnight, then carry on partying until the doors close much, much later.

Teatro Greco

Via Teatro Greco 40; freephone 800 542; www.indofondazione.org
Nothing beats a classical drama set in Taormina's stunning Greek Theatre, and visitors come from around the world for the annual summer arts festival in July and August. Performances include classical drama, opera, dance and music. Plays are staged in the original language. The theatre is the setting for screenings during the Taormina Film Fest (www.taorminafilmfest.it) in mid-June.

Catania

Mercati Generali

SS417 Caltagirone to Gela; tel: 095 571 458; www.mercatigenerali.org
This converted warehouse set amid orange groves is a cult music venue. It's one of the few clubs in Sicily where you'll find top European DJs, live rock and pop. Summer partying in the courtyard hots up from around midnight nightly in summer. It's not an easy spot to get to, involving a 20-minute taxi ride from Catania.

Teatro Massimo Bellini

Via Perrotta 12; tel: 095 730 6110; www.teatromassimobellini.it
Named after the famous operatic composer Bellini, the theatre opened in 1890 with his opera *Norma*. It's a major venue for opera, classical music and ballet. Tickets (available online) are highly sought after, especially for operas composed by Bellini himself.

Zò

Piazzale Asia 6; tel: 095 816 8912; www.zoculture.com
This futuristic new culture and arts centre, housed in an ex-sulphur refinery near Stazione Centrale, hosts concerts, films, club nights, cutting-edge theatre and offbeat art exhibitions. Some events are free of charge. The centre is also home to two small museums, one dedicated to Catania's early 20th-century film industry, the other to the Allied invasion of Sicily in 1943.

Sicilian elder

A–Z

A

Age restrictions

According to Italian law, persons under 16 are not allowed to drink alcohol. The minimum age for driving with a valid licence is 18, but for renting a car in most cases a driver must be 25 or over.

B

Budgeting for your trip

Prices generally match those of mainland Italy. Mid-range hotels charge €150–200 a night for a double room, and you can pay more than €400 at a luxury hotel. B&Bs and *agriturismi* are much cheaper. In touristy areas you'll find a three-course dinner with wine will set you back €40-plus a head, but simple *trattorie* charge much less. Fuel costs are similar to those across Europe, but public transport remains comfortably inexpensive. A taxi from Palermo airport to the city centre costs €40, from Catania €25–30. EU citizens over 65 or under 18 are allowed free entry to many sights, and those from 18 to 25 get a 50 percent discount.

C

Children

Children are always made to feel welcome, and are readily accepted in res-

taurants. Although restaurants don't often have kids' menus, any restaurant will happily prepare a simple pasta with cheese or tomato sauce for the little ones. You can also ask for half portions. At the beach, children usually wear bathing suits and it is not customary to let them run around naked if they are over two years old. Babysitting services are available in many of the upper-range hotels. Children under the age of six are usually admitted to sights free of charge and those from six to 16 at 50 percent discount.

Climate

April, May, September and October are the loveliest months, when Sicily enjoys a semblance of solitude combined with the pleasures of a mild climate. July and August, on the opposite, are crowded with Italian and foreign tourists and temperatures can get very hot. If going to the beach is not your main concern, going in winter may also be an option: there's a lot to see and temperatures are mild with relatively frequent sunny days.

Clothing

Bring light clothing and a hat during the hot summer months. In spring (April and May) and autumn (October and November) you will need a jacket or sweater

Caltagirone steps

for the evenings. Winters, particularly in the mountainous central areas, can be cold. Mount Etna requires strong footwear in any season.

Crime and safety

Petty crime is the main problem for tourists: pickpocketing, bag-snatching and theft from cars, particularly in Palermo, Catania and the historic centre of Siracusa. Keep an eye on valuables at all times, and when driving always lock car doors and keep valuables hidden. If you are robbed, report it as soon as possible to the local police. You will need a copy of the declaration in order to claim on your insurance.

Customs

Free exchange of non-duty-free goods for personal use is allowed between EU countries. For non-EU citizens the duty-free allowances are 200 cigarettes, 50 cigars, 1 litre of spirits, 2 litres of wine, 60ml of perfume, 250ml of eau de toilette, and duty-free gifts worth up to €175.

D

Disabled travellers

Sicily is one of the worst places in Italy to get around for disabled travellers. Most churches and sites have steps, and few of the museums and archaeological sites have wheelchair access.

Given the challenges, it is wisest to book through a specialised tour operator who can offer customised tours and itineraries, eg www.flyingwheels travel.com and Accessible Journeys (www.disabilitytravel.com). Access-Able Travel Source (www.access-able.com) is a database of travel agents from around the world with experience in accessible travel.

E

Electricity

Sockets take two or three round-pronged plugs; supplies are 220-volts AC, 50 cycles. Your best bet is to bring a travel adaptor with you. Adaptors can be bought before you leave home, or at airports and stations.

Embassies and consulates

If your passport is lost or stolen you will need to obtain a police report and have proof of your identity to get a new one. Then call your consulate in Rome (see below):

Australian Embassy: Via Antonio Bosio 5; tel: 06 852 721; www.italy.embassy. gov.au

Canadian Embassy: Via Zara 30; tel: 06 8544 43937; www.canada.it

Irish Embassy: Piazza Campitelli 3; tel: 06 595 2381; www.ambasciata-irlanda.it

UK Embassy: Via XX Settembre 80a; tel: 06 4220 0001; www.gov.uk/government/world/italy.it

US Embassy: Via Vittorio Veneto 121; tel: 06 46741; www.usembassy.it

Fishing in Palermo

Emergencies

General emergences: 113; Police: 112; Fire: 115: Ambulance: 118; Breakdown/ road assistance: 116

Etiquette

Wearing miniskirts, skimpy shorts or shoulderless garments in churches is likely to cause offence. Casual clothes are quite acceptable in most restaurants, but avoid swimwear. If invited for dinner by locals, you are expected to always bring something: pastries, wine or flowers are always appreciated.

G

Gay and lesbian travellers

Many gay travellers report having been the object of negative comments when displaying affection in public, but attitudes are fairly relaxed in the bigger cities, where gay magazines are sold at most newsstands. Taormina is still the focus for the native and foreign gay community. Consult Arci-gay, the national gay rights organisation, www.arcigay.it, or contact the Palermo branch (tel: 349 884 5809; email: palermo@arcigay.it). To access bars and discos, you need to join the association.

Green issues

Sicily's record on recycling is poor to say the least (piles of rubbish are a familiar sight), and a new project for waste man-

agement is frozen for lack of finances. Although the larger centres have bikes to rent and a few hotels have free bikes, urban leisure cycling has yet to take off. A bike scheme set up in Ortigia failed after all the new ranks were permanently vandalised.

Several specialist companies offer bike tours in rural Sicily and the islands, eg Sole&Bike (www.solebike.it). Beautiful stretches of coastline and mountain regions are now protected as nature reserves, attracting cyclists and hikers, and the island has seen an increasing number of sustainable tourism projects created in recent years.

For ideas on accommodation and green stays in Sicily, visit Responsible Travel (www.responsibletravel. com), which promotes eco, green and responsible holidays.

H

Health

All EU countries have reciprocal arrangements for medical services. UK residents should obtain a European Health Insurance Card. This only covers medical care, not emergency repatriation costs or additional expenses. It is therefore advisable, and for non-EU residents essential, to have travel insurance to cover all eventualities.

In many areas in summer there is a *Guardia Medica Turistica* (tourist emergency medical service) which functions 24 hours a day. Details are available

Lípari at dusk   *Trápani dog*

from pharmacies, tourist offices and hotels.

Pharmacies and hospitals

A pharmacy (*farmacia*) is identified by a green cross. All main towns offer a 24-hour pharmacy service, with a night-time and Sunday rota. Duty pharmacists are posted on all pharmacy doors and published in the daily papers. For emergencies, dial 118 for an ambulance or head for the *Pronto Soccorso* (Accident and Emergency) of the local hospital.

I

Internet facilities

Internet cafés and points, which come and go, can be found in towns and resorts. To use them you may need to show a passport or EU identity card. Wi-Fi hotspots are scant, but many hotels now have Wi-Fi access.

L

Left luggage

Luggage can be left at the left-luggage office at Palermo's Stazione Centrale (daily 7am–11pm) and at Stazione Marittima (daily 7am–7.30pm).

Lost property

In the event of lost luggage on a train, go to the left luggage office at Stazione Centrale. Items lost in the street are never recovered.

Media

The main Italian papers (*Corriere della Sera* and *La Repubblica*) publish southern editions, but the local dailies are more popular. *Il Giornale di Sicilia*, Palermo's paper, covers western Sicily, and includes practical listings. *La Sicilia*, Catania's main paper, also has provincial supplements for Siracusa, Ragusa and Enna. The major towns and resorts have English-language newspapers the following day.

Money

Currency

The currency in Italy is the euro (€). A euro is divided into 100 cents with 5, 20 and 50 cent coins, and 1 and 2 euro coins. The euro notes are 5, 10, 20, 50, 100, 200 and 500.

Changing money

You will need your passport or identification card when changing money, which can be a slow operation. Not all banks will provide cash against a credit card, and some may refuse to cash travellers' cheques in certain currencies. On the whole, the larger banks (those with a national or international network) will be the best for tourist transactions.

Credit cards

Except in smaller villages, major credit cards are accepted by shops, hotels,

Sampling the delights at this pasticceria in Erice

restaurants and petrol stations. They can also be used to pay motorway tolls, but it's always best to also keep some cash on hand, as the card-reading machines are frequently out of order.

Cash machines

ATMs (*bancomats* in Italian) are found all over the island, even in small towns. Instructions are given in English. They are the easiest and generally the cheapest way to obtain cash.

Taxes

Italy imposes VAT (IVA) on most goods and services, including hotels. Non-EU citizens are entitled to a refund of around 12 percent if they spend over €155 at stores with a 'Tax Free for Tourists' sign. The invoice must be stamped at Customs; you then receive the rebate when you go to the Tax Free desk at the airport.

Tipping

A 10–15 percent service charge is often included in restaurant bills, and although a tip will be appreciated, no extra is expected. For quick service in bars, leave a coin or two extra. Round up the fare for taxi drivers, and tip guides €5 per person.

O

Opening hours

Shops are generally open 9am–1pm and 4–7.30pm. Except for those in tour-

ist resorts, shops are closed on Sundays. Food shops may also close on Wednesday afternoons. In cities, other shops are closed on Monday mornings.

Banks are open Mon–Fri 8.30am–1.20pm. Some also open from 2.45–4pm.

Post offices are open weekdays from 8.30am–1.15pm, Saturdays from 8.30–11.20am.

P

Police

Emergency telephone numbers: Police 112, General emergency services 113. The Carabinieri, in blue uniforms, are the armed military police who handle public law and order; the Polizia Stradale, or state police, patrol the highways and other roads.

Post

The postal service is notoriously slow. If you need to send an urgent letter, send it by Postacelere. Post offices are generally open Mon–Sat 8.30am–1.30pm, with main post offices in the cities staying open all day. In Palermo the main post office in Via Roma (near Piazza Domenico) is open Mon–Sat 8am–6.30pm. Stamps are also available from tobacconists (*tabacchi*) and bars that also sell cigarettes. Italian postboxes are red and have two slots, *per la città* (for the local city/town) and *per tutte le alter destinazioni* (for all other destinations).

Chiesa del Gesù, Palermo

Public holidays

Banks and most shops are closed on the following holidays:

1 January: New Year's Day
6 January: Epiphany
March/April: Easter Monday
25 April: Liberation Day
1 May: May Day
2 June: Republic Day
15 August: Ferragosto; Assumption Day
1 November: All Saints' Day
8 December: Feast of the Immaculate Conception
25 December: Christmas Day
26 December: Boxing Day

Major holidays and festivals

New Year's Eve is very big business in Sicily: there is usually a large dinner followed by drinking, dancing and firecrackers. It falls in the middle of a long holiday period that begins on Christmas Eve and lasts until Epiphany on 6 January. The friendly witch *(befana)* who brings candy to the good kids and coal to the naughty ones is a strongly felt tradition in Italy and especially in Southern Italy. Easter is normally a three or four-day religious holiday, though businesses only close on Easter Sunday and Monday. Trápani is famous for its Easter procession, when 20 life-size wooden statues, dating from the 18th century, are paraded for 10 hours through the streets. The statues, or *Misteri*, are kept in the

Chiesa del Purgatorio on Via Francesco d'Assisi (which unfortunately is usually closed).

Every city or town has its own patron Saint, celebrated with processions around the city centre, some of which end with suggestive ceremonies by the sea.

R

Religion

Italy is a Catholic country. The hours of Mass vary, but each church has its own Mass timetable pinned on its main door.

Other denominations may practise their faith without hindrance and have their own services in Palermo and Catania.

S

Smoking

Smoking is banned in public places, including bars and restaurants. A few establishments have special smoking rooms, and outdoor ones allow smoking.

T

Telephones

Several companies provide public payphones that accept phone cards *(scheda telefonica)* or coins. You can buy cards in various denominations from *tabacchi* and from many newsstands. Some payphones, especially in airports, accept credit cards, but

fares can be high. There are a number of inexpensive international calling cards available from newsstands and call centres (in the bigger cities, usually around the train stations) where you can make a call and pay later.

For calls within Italy, telephone numbers must be preceded by the area code even if the call is made within the same district.

When phoning abroad from Italy dial 00 (the international access code), then the country code, followed by the city or area code omitting the initial 0, and then the desired number.

International dialling codes are (44) for the UK, (353) for Ireland, (61) for Australia and (1) for US and Canada.

For international directory enquiries and operator-assisted national and international calls, call 892-412.

Mobile phone numbers begin with 3, for example 338, 340, 333, 348, and cost a lot more.

Mobile (Cell) phones

Check the international roaming rates with your company prior to departure, and whether your phone can receive and make calls in Italy.

Maximum roaming rates are regulated by the European Commission, however if you are going to make a large number of calls or staying in Italy for some time it may be worth purchasing a SIM 'pay as you go' card, available at shops of the main provider or at the post office.

Time zones

Italy and Sicily follow Central European Time (GMT+1) but, from the last Sunday in March to the last Sunday in October, the clocks advance one additional hour to become GMT+2. This means in summer when it is noon in Sicily it will be 11am in London and 6am in New York.

Toilets

Public toilets are hard to find, but you can usually use toilets in cafés and bars. In many cases the toilets are locked and you will have to ask for the key *(chiave)* at the till. Buying a drink at the same time will be appreciated. Major sites now have reasonable facilities.

Tourist information

Most of the main tourist offices will have staff who speak foreign languages, but this is often not the case with smaller information offices. If you can't find a tourist office, try a travel agency or local tour operator, as these can be good sources of advice.

Agrigento: Via Empedocle, 73; tel: 0922 20391
Catania: Via Vittorio Emanuele II 172; tel: 095 742557; www.turismo. catania.it
Cefalù: Corso Ruggero 77; tel: 0921 421050
Lípari: Corso Vittorio Emanuele, 202; tel: 090 988 0095

Excursion boat in Milazzo

Palermo (city and province): Piazza Castelnuovo 34; tel: 091 605 8351; www.palermotourism.com

Siracusa: Via Roma 31, Ortigia; tel: 800 055500, and Via Maestranza 33; tel: 0931 464255

Taormina: Palazzo Corvaja, Piazza Santa Caterina; tel: 0942 23243

Trápani: Info Point, Via San Grancesco d'Assisi 27; tel: 0923 806 8008; www.apt.trapani.it

Transport

Arriving by air

Sicily currently has three international airports: Palermo (Falcone-Borsellino), Catania (Fontanarossa) and Trápani (Birgi). A new airport, Comiso, close to Ragusa, was completed in Spring 2013. Travellers for Messina use the Reggio di Calabria airport on the Italian mainland, just across the Strait of Messina.

The islands of **Lampedusa** and **Pantelleria** are linked by air services from Palermo or Trápani.

Palermo Airport

Palermo's Falcone-Borsellino airport (www.gesap.it) is 30km (19 miles) west of the capital at Punta Raisi. It is used by all the major airlines. Bus services run daily from 5.30am every 30 minutes, linking the airport with Palermo's Piazza Politeama and the central train station. Tickets can be purchased on the bus, and the journey takes around an hour. The Trinacria Express train service also runs every half-hour from the airport to the central station, taking

55 minutes, and is a fraction cheaper than the bus.

Catania Airport

Catania's Fontanarossa airport (www.aeroporto.catania.it) is 5km (3 miles) south of the city. There is an Alibus service departing every 20 minutes for Stazione Centrale (the central railway station), taking 20 minutes. Tickets can be bought from a newsstand inside the terminal. Services run by Interbus (www.interbus.it) link the airport to Siracusa, Ragusa, Taormina and many other cities in eastern Sicily, as well as Palermo.

Comiso Airport (Ragusa)

The Vincenzo Magliocco airport (www.aeroportodicomiso.com) serves Comiso and Ragusa and is used to complement Catania's Fontanarossa airport with charter and low-cost flights to some of Europe's most important destinations, including Stansted, Dublin, Frankfurt. Various private bus and coach lines, such as Autolinee Giamporcaro, Autolinee Tumino, Etna Trasporti and AST link it to Ragusa and surrounding towns and to the Catania airport.

Trápani Airport

Trápani-Birgi's Vincenzo Florio airport (www.airgest.it), used by low-cost carriers, is 15km (9 miles) southeast of Trápani. AST buses link the airport to Trápani every half-hour, taking 25 minutes, with connections to Palermo, Agrigento and Marsala. Terravision coaches (www.terravision.eu) to Palermo link up with Ryanair flights.

Arriving by rail

The Italian mainland is linked to Sicily by train, with Milan, Rome and Naples the best connecting stations to the south. Unfortunately, the great improvements in the Italian rail system do not extend to Sicily, and the overnight sleeper service from Sicily to northern Italy has been cancelled.

There is a daily service between Rome and Palermo, Catania and Siracusa. At the crossing from Villa San Giovanni on the Italian peninsula the train carriages are shunted into the ferry, and then shunted off again at Messina. Palermo's main station is Stazione Centrale. Always book a seat for long-distance travel.

For information and online booking visit the Trenitalia website (www.trenitalia.com) or call tel: 892021 (toll number, expect long waits). Tickets can be picked up (or bought directly) from one of the self-service machines at the station.

Arriving by sea

Ferries link Sicily with Naples, Genova (Genoa), Salerno and Civitavecchia in Italy and with Cagliari in Sardinia; there are also links with Tunis in Tunisia and Malta.

Hydrofoils *(aliscafi)* operate between Sicily and its smaller islands (see under Transport within Sicily below). Sicily can be combined with Malta on a two-island holiday using Virtu Ferries (www.virtu ferries.com).

Ferry tickets can be booked online (though there is no need for the Messina/Villa San Giovanni crossing). The main operators are SNAV (www.snav.it), Grandi Navi Veloci (www.gnv.it), Tirrenia (www.tirrenia.it) and Grimaldi (www.grimaldi-lines.com). There are cabins on the longer routes, and these must be booked well in advance for high summer. Remember that sailing schedules are prone to change, especially in winter months when the seas can turn rough.

Arriving by car

Driving to Sicily from the UK takes 24 hours. Even from Rome it is a good seven hours to Villa San Giovanni in Calabria, where you cross to Sicily. To bring a car into Italy you will need a current driving licence and valid insurance. You must carry your driving licence, car registration, insurance documents and passport with you at all times when driving. You are also required to carry a triangular warning sign and a high visibility vest.

Transport around Sicily

Driving

A car in Sicily is a great help exploring the island, though in cities like Palermo, Catania or Siracusa, it is easier and less nerve-racking to use public transport or taxis. The network of roads has much improved, though you can still expect potholes even on some of the major roads. A system of mainly toll-free

Easy-going Sicilians

motorways *(autostrade)* crosses parts of the island, linking the main cities. Elsewhere roads can be quite slow-going, especially in the mountainous regions.

The main frustrations of driving in Sicily are parking (see below), negotiating town centres (which often have complex one-way systems and poor signing to the centre), Sicilian motorists who drive too fast and frequently recklessly, and the huge distances you have to drive to see the spread-out highlights of the island.

Car hire

Major hire companies include Avis, Europcar, Hertz and Sixt. You'll find offices in the main airports, but it's usually cheaper to book ahead through major travel websites or specialists such as www.auto-europe.co.uk.

Drivers must present their own national driving licence. Credit-card imprints are taken as a deposit and are usually the only form of payment acceptable. 'Inclusive' prices do not generally include personal accident insurance or insurance against damage to windscreens, tyres and wheels. Pay attention to your return time – it's easy to get charged for an extra day.

Rules and regulations

Drive on the right, pass on the left. Speed limits are 50km/h (30mph) in towns and built-up areas, 90km/h (55mph) on main roads and 130km/h (80mph) on motorways. Speeding and other traffic offences are subject to heavy on-the-spot fines.

The use of hand-held mobiles while driving is prohibited. The blood alcohol limit is 0.05 percent, and police occasionally make random breath tests. Seat belts are compulsory in the front and back. Lights must be used on all out-of-town roads.

Parking

Finding a parking space in town centres is notoriously tricky. Historic centres are often inaccessible to cars, other than those of residents, though visitors staying at hotels with parking facilities are allowed access. Look for a white 'P' on a blue background for parking lots and garages at the fringes of the town centre. Elsewhere in towns parking is controlled by meters or scratch cards, available from tobacconists and bars. Illegal parking valets *(parcheggiatori abusive)* are very common in the big centres and on the coast, and will ask you for a euro or two to 'protect' your car, often without helping you park at all. When they do, they may suggest that you park in a no-parking area, saying that it's OK to park there or that they are friends with the police officers, so it is advisable to read the signs independently before deciding to trust them.

Fuel

Petrol *(benzina)* is readily available, and there are many 24-hour stations with self-service dispensers that accept euro notes and credit cards, though it's wise to always bring cash in case the credit card machine is out

Friendly face

of order. For unleaded ask for *senza piombo*.

Rail

Trains are operated by Italian State Railways, Ferrovie dello Stato (www.trenitalia.com). The rail system in Sicily is cheap but slow, and not really convenient for seeing all of the island.

The east of the island is better linked than the west. Messina is well linked to both Palermo and Catania, and all trains to Italy pass through its port in order to cross the Strait of Messina by ferry.

Catania is linked with the major cities (though trains take twice as long from here to Palermo as the coach) and is the starting point of the Ferrovia Circumetnea, the narrow-gauge train that calls at all villages around Mount Etna on a circular route (see page 85).

Seat reservations are obligatory on the faster Intercity services. Tickets for all trains must be stamped in the yellow machines on the platforms before boarding the train.

Taxi

In cities, taxis are best telephoned or found at taxi ranks in the main squares of the larger towns. Licensed taxis are white, with a Taxi sign on the roof, and have a meter which should be turned on at the start of the journey. When it comes to tipping, it's usual to round up the fare. Beware of touts without meters who may approach you at airports and large train stations.

Palermo: Radio Taxi: tel: 091 513 311, 091 513 198.

Catania: Radio Taxi: tel: 095 330 966.

Coach and bus

Fast bus services link Sicily's main towns and offer relatively speedy access to the interior and the south. Generally speaking, coaches are more reliable and quicker than trains, but they cost more.

City buses have a flat fare and tickets are valid for 75 minutes, including change of bus routes. Bus tickets, available from bars, tobacconists, and from machines at bus terminals and metro stations, must be validated in the machine on the bus.

Ferries/hydrofoils

Getting to the Aeolian Islands. Access by ferry and hydrofoil to the islands is shortest and most frequent from Milazzo (near Messina) on the north coast, accessed by the A19 and A20 autostrada from Palermo or A20 from Messina, or by train from both cities. In the summer, there are up to 11 hydrofoils a day to Lípari and Vulcano, and six a day to Salina. In high season some boats also go from Messina, Cefalù and Palermo. Hydrofoils are faster and slightly more expensive, but ferries give you better views. Services, which are quite often suspended due to bad weather, are run by Ustica Lines (www.usticalines.it), Siremar (www.siremar.it) and NGI (www.ngi-spa.it).

Getting to the Egadi Islands. Ferries and hydrofoils from Trápani run several times a day to the Egadi Islands (Favig-

Catania market

nana, Lévanzo and Maréttimo). Ferries are mainly operated by Siremar (www.siremar.it) and Uscita Lines (www.ustica lines.it).

V

Visas and passports

Visas are not required by visitors from EU countries. A current passport or valid Identification Card is sufficient. For visitors from the US, Canada, Australia or New Zealand a visa is not required, but a valid passport is essential for entry to be granted for a stay of up to three months. Nationals of most other countries require a visa. This must be obtained in advance from an Italian Embassy or Consulate.

W

Wine resort tours

Sicily has seen an increasing number of appealing wine estates where visitors can usually also spend the night, dine or do a cookery or wine-tasting course. Just outside Alcamo, the Sirignano Wine Resort is a delightful organic estate run by the Marchese de Gregorio (www.sirignanowineresort.it). Guests stay in converted farmworkers' cottages and sample the superb wines over meals cooked by an outstanding chef. For more comprehensive guided tours through Sicily's wine tradition, visitors can contact a number of wine tour companies: Wine Tours in Sicily (www.winetourinsicily.com) and Italy and Wine (www.italyandwine.it) are two of the most popular ones.

Websites

Websites for specific sights and other attractions are given throughout the book. Other useful sites are:

www.enit.it. Italy's official tourism website, with information about the most important sights.

www.regione.sicilia.it/turismo. Official Sicilian tourist website. Go to 'La Sicilia per il Turista' on the home page for tourist information in English.

www.yourwaytosicilia.com. Official Sicilian tourist office website.

www.parks.it. Italian parks and reserves (then consult Sicily).

www.bestofsicily.com. Packed with information; strong on culture.

Women

Women travellers will invariably come across Sicilians with a roving eye, but serious harassment and sexual assaults are rare. Use common sense (eg avoid scanty clothing in towns), and beware of bag-snatchers and pickpockets. In some of the smaller internal towns it is unusual to see women sitting at a bar alone, and that may attract attention. After dark it is wise to avoid the unlit backstreets in Palermo and Catania and the Via Nizza port area of Siracusa. The resorts of Taormina and Cefalù are normally extremely safe.

Sicilians love to chat

LANGUAGE

Italian is relatively easy to pick up, if you have any knowledge of French or Spanish (or a grounding in Latin). Most hotels have staff who speak some English, and unless you go well off the beaten track, you should have little problem communicating in shops or restaurants. However, there are places not on the tourist circuit where you will have the chance to practise your Italian, and local people will think more of you for making an effort. Here are a few basics to help you get started.

General
Yes *Sì*
No *No*
Thank you *Grazie*
Many thanks *Mille grazie/Tante grazie*
You're welcome *Prego*
All right/That's fine *Va bene*
Please *Per favore/Per cortesia*
Excuse me (to get attention) *Scusi*
Excuse me (in a crowd) *Permesso*
Could you help me? (formal) *Potrebbe aiutarmi?*
Certainly *Ma, certo/Certamente*
Can you show me...? *Può indicarmi...?*
Can you help me, please? *Può aiutarmi, per cortesia?*
I need... *Ho bisogno di...*
I'm lost *Mi sono perso*
I'm sorry *Mi dispiace*

I don't know *Non lo so*
I don't understand *Non capisco*
Do you speak English/French/Spanish? *Parla inglese/francese/spagnolo?*
Could you speak more slowly? *Può parlare più lentamente, per favore?*
Could you repeat that please? *Può ripetere, per piacere?*
How much does it cost? *quanto costa?*
this one/that one *questo/quello*
Have you got...? *Avete...?*

At a bar/restaurant
I'd like to book a table *Vorrei prenotare un tavolo*
Have you got a table for... *Avete un tavolo per...*
I have a reservation *Ho prenotato*
lunch *il pranzo*
supper *la cena*
I'm a vegetarian *Sono vegetariano/a*
May we have the menu? *Ci dia la carta?*
What would you like? *Che cosa prende?*
I'd like... *Vorrei...*
mineral water *acqua minerale*
fizzy/still *gasata/naturale*
a bottle of *una bottiglia di*
a glass of *un bicchieri di*
red wine *vino rosso*
white wine *vino bianco*
beer *una birra*

Numbers
One *uno*
Two *due*

Classic cars

Three *tre*
Four *quattro*
Five *cinque*
Six *sei*
Seven *sette*
Eight *otto*
Nine *nove*
Ten *dieci*
Twenty *venti*
Thirty *trenta*
Forty *quaranta*
Fifty *cinquanta*
One hundred *cento*
One thousand *mille*

Getting around

What time do you open/close? *A che ora apre/chiude?*
Closed for the holidays *Chiuso per ferie*
Where can I buy tickets? *Dove posso fare i biglietti?*
What time does the train leave? *A che ora parte il treno?*
Can you tell me where to get off? *Mi può dire dove devo scendere?*
Where is the nearest bank/hotel? *Dov'è la banca/l'albergo più vicino?*
On the right *a destra*
On the left *a sinistra*
Go straight on *Va sempre diritto*

Online

Where's an internet cafe? *Dov'è un Internet caffè?*
Does it have wireless internet? *C'è il wireless?*
What is the WiFi password? *Qual è la password Wi-Fi?*
Is the WiFi free? *Il WiFi è gratis?*
How do I turn the computer on/off? *Come si accende/spegne il computer?*
Can I...? *Posso...?*
access the internet *collegarmi (a Internet)*
check e-mail *controllare le e-mail*
print *stampare*
plug in/charge my laptop/iPhone/iPad? *collegare/ricaricare il mio portatile/iPhone/iPad?*
access Skype? *usare Skype?*
How much per hour/half hour? *Quanto costa per un'ora/mezz'ora?*
How do I...? *Come...?*
connect/disconnect *ci si collega/scollega*
log on/log off *si fa il login/logout*
What's your e-mail? *Qual è la sua e-mail?*
My e-mail is... *La mia e-mail è...*

Social media

Are you on Facebook/Twitter? *È su Facebook/Twitter? (polite form) Sei su Facebook/Twitter? (informal form)*
What's your user name? *Qual è il suo nome utente? (polite form) Qual è il tuo nome utente? (informal form)*
I'll add you as a friend. *La aggiungerò come amico. (polite form) Ti aggiungerò come amico. (informal form)*
I'll follow you on Twitter. *La seguirò su Twitter. (polite form) Ti seguirò su Twitter. (informal form)*
I'll put the pictures on Facebook/Twitter. *Metterò le foto su Facebook/Twitter.*

Taormina's Teatro Greco hosts an array of cultural events

BOOKS AND FILM

With its rural areas, its beauty and its history, Sicily has inspired many authors and film directors. The Mafia, with its mysteries and crime stories, has also had an important role in literature and cinema, giving Sicily a type of fame the Sicilians would have been happier without.

Books

History and culture
The Leopard, by Giuseppe Tomasi di Lampedusa. This is both the classic Sicilian novel and one of the most important novels in Italian literature.

The Last Leopard: A Life of Giuseppe Tomasi di Lampedusa, by David Gilmour. This is a sensitive literary biography and companion to *The Leopard* itself, based on interviews with the author's adopted son and full access to the family archives.

The Normans in Sicily, by John Julius Norwich. This remains the best introduction to the "other" Norman Conquest, including of Southern Italy and Sicily – led by the great Euro-adventurers.

Cavalleria Rusticana and Other Stories, I Malavoglia, History of a Capinera, by Giovanni Verga. One of Italy's most important authors, Verga was a realist writer best known for his depictions of rural Sicily and poverty. His most famous novel is *Cavalleria Rusticana*.

Fredrick II: A Medieval Emperor, by David Abulafia. A biography of Fredrick II.

Crime and society
The Shape of Water, The Terracotta Dog, The Voice of the Violin and **The Snack Thief**, by Andrea Camilleri. These detective stories/thrillers are worldwide best-sellers, helped by the Montalbano films.

Boss of Bosses, by Clare Longrigg. This account covers the role and importance of Bernardo Provenzano, the Mafia boss *(capo di tutti capi)* who was arrested in 2006 in Corleone.

The Day of the Owl, by Leonardo Sciascia. This novel about the Mafia was written by a rigorous writer and politician (1921–83) often known as 'the conscience of Sicily'.

Midnight in Sicily, by Peter Robb. Personal insights and trenchant observations on Sicilian society, customs, relationships, art, food, history and the Mafia.

No Questions Asked, by Clare Longrigg. This account covers the varied role of women in the Cosa Nostra, whom the author persuaded to talk.

Travel and general
Bagheria, by Dacia Maraini. The author, the daughter of a Sicilian princess, revisits the family's ancestral villa in Bagheria, in an attempt to come to terms with her past and with the desecration of this once glorious town.

Bitter Almonds, by Mary Taylor Simeti and Maria Grammatico. This foodie

Romantic Ortigia   *Ingrid Bergman during the filming of Stromboli*

memoir is inspired by a disappearing Sicily, linked to the convents producing pastries, notably the almond pastries in Erice.

Clay Ghosts in Sicily, by Angie Voluti. Set in post-war Palermo, this quirky new novel features a lovelorn young Sicilian sculptress haunted by memories conjured up by visits to the capital, with its secret tunnels and dilapidated palaces.

Good Girls Don't Wear Trousers, by Lara Cardella. Living in a stifling Sicilian town in the early 1960s, teenage Annetta dreams that wearing trousers will give her freedom.

A House in Sicily, by Daphne Phelps. An affectionate travel memoir centred on Casa Cuseni, a Taormina pensione that welcomed artists and writers such as Tennessee Williams and Roald Dahl.

Made in Sicily, Giorgio Locatelli. This new gastronomic tour of Sicily presents the celebrity chef's simplest yet most authentic island recipes.

The Silent Duchess, by Dacia Maraini. Set in the mid-18th century, this novel tells of a noble family, seen through the eyes of the deaf-mute duchess.

Films

Cabiria (1914). A silent film set in ancient Sicily during the Punic Wars.

Cinema Paradiso (1988). Flashbacks of the protagonist's childhood give a glimpse of Sicily in the 1950s to the soundtrack of Ennio Morricone.

Divorce, Italian Style (*Divorzio all'italiana*; 1961). This comedy by Pietro Germi portrays passion and romantic relationships in 1960s Sicily.

The Postman (*Il Postino*; 1994). The story of an exiled poet who lives in Lampedusa, and of his friendship with his postman (Massimo Troisi) who learns to love poetry.

The Star Maker (*L'Uomo delle Stelle*; 1995). This film by Giuseppe Tornatore tells the story of a fake movie director who travels rural Sicily, offering to shoot screen test of aspiring actors.

The Leopard (*Il Gattopardo*; 1968). Luchino Visconti's take on Tomasi de Lampedusa's famous novel.

Stromboli (1949). This movie by Roberto Rossellini depicts the culture and mentality of the inhabitants of Stromboli from the eyes of a displaced Lithuanian woman who moves there after the war.

The Godfather (1972). Francis Ford Coppola's American crime story tells the story of the fictional Corleone Mafia family.

Johnny Stecchino (1991). An entertaining comedy in which bus driver Dante (Roberto Benigni) is mistaken for a fierce Mafia gangster.

L'Avventura (1960). A young woman disappears during a boating trip. While searching for her, her lover and her best friend fall in love.

The Big Blue (1988). Luc Besson's fictionalised account of the sporting rivalry between two free divers. The World Diving Championship scenes were filmed in Taormina.

ABOUT THIS BOOK

This *Explore Guide* has been produced by the editors of Insight Guides, whose books have set the standard for visual travel guides since 1970. With top-quality photography and authoritative recommendations, these guidebooks bring you the very best routes and itineraries in the world's most exciting destinations.

BEST ROUTES

The routes in the book provide something to suit all budgets, tastes and trip lengths. As well as covering the destination's many classic attractions, the itineraries track lesser-known sights. The routes embrace a range of interests, so whether you are an art fan, a gourmet, a history buff or have kids to entertain, you will find an option to suit.

We recommend reading the whole of a route before setting out. This should help you to familiarise yourself with it and enable you to plan where to stop for refreshments – options are shown in the 'Food and Drink' box at the end of each tour.

For our pick of the tours by theme, consult Recommended Routes for… (see pages 4–5).

INTRODUCTION

The routes are set in context by this introductory section, giving an overview of the destination to set the scene, plus background information on food and drink, shopping and more, while a succinct history timeline highlights the key events over the centuries.

DIRECTORY

Also supporting the routes is a Directory chapter, with a clearly organised A–Z of practical information, our pick of where to stay while you are there and select restaurant listings; these eateries complement the more low-key cafés and restaurants that feature within the routes and are intended to offer a wider choice for evening dining. Also included here are some nightlife listings, plus a handy language guide and our recommendations for books and films about the destination.

ABOUT THE AUTHORS

Susie Boulton's passion for Sicily was born when she visited the island whilst studying History of Art at Cambridge University. Since then she has written some 25 guidebooks, mostly focussing on Italy. **Lisa Gerard-Sharp** is an award-winning travel writer and Italy specialist who has written numerous Insight Guides as well as contributing to newspapers, magazines and television. A Rome-based foreign affairs journalist, **Daniel Mosseri** is also a passionate explorer and has travelled to Sicily extensively. In his many trips, he has fallen in love with every single layer of the island's art history, but also with its pastries and its vegetation.

CONTACT THE EDITORS

We hope you find this Explore Guide useful, interesting and a pleasure to read. If you have any questions or feedback on the text, pictures or maps, please do let us know. If you have noticed any errors or outdated facts, or have suggestions for places to include on the routes, we would be delighted to hear from you. Please drop us an email at insight@apaguide.co.uk. Thanks!

CREDITS

Explore Sicily
Contributors: Susie Boulton, Lisa Gerard-Sharp and Daniel Mosseri
Commissioning Editor: Carine Tracanelli
Series Editor: Sarah Clark
Pictures/Art: Tom Smyth/Shahid Mahmood
Map Production: originial cartography Stephen Ramsay, updated by Apa Cartography Department
Production: Tynan Dean and Rebeka Davies
Photo credits: Bigstock 10, 27, 85, 89L, 90; Caol Ishka 104; Corbis 137; Domenico Palace 106, 118/119; Dreamstime 15, 16/17, 56/57, 62, 75L, 94/95, 95, 110, 112/113, 116/117, 117; Fotolia 52, 66/67, 110/111; Grand Hotel Timeo 98, 106/107, 107; Insight Guides 5T, 5ML, 5MR, 6MR, 11, 65, 70; iStockphoto 18, 28MC, 100/101, 104/105, 108, 109, 112, 116; Kempinski Giardino di Costanza 102, 102/103; La Madia 114, 114/115, 115; Neil Buchan-Grant/Apa Publications 1, 2ML, 2MC, 2MR, 2MR, 2MC, 2ML, 2/3T, 4TL, 4MC, 4ML, 4BC, 5M, 6ML, 6MC, 6ML, 6MR, 6/7T, 8, 8/9, 9, 10/11, 12, 12/13, 13, 14, 14/15, 18/19, 19, 20, 20/21, 21, 22/23, 24, 24/25, 25, 26, 28ML, 28MC, 28MR, 28ML, 28MR, 28/29T, 30, 30/31, 32, 32/33, 34, 34/35, 36, 36/37, 37, 38, 38/39, 39, 40, 40/41, 41, 42, 42/43, 44, 44/45, 45, 46, 46/47, 47, 48, 48/49, 50, 50/51, 51, 52/53, 54, 54/55, 55, 58/59, 60, 60/61, 61, 62/63, 64, 64/65, 66, 68, 68/69, 69, 70/71, 71, 72, 73, 72/73, 74, 74/75, 76, 76/77, 77, 78, 78/79, 79, 80, 80/81, 82, 82/83, 83, 84, 86, 86/87, 87, 88, 88/89, 90/91, 92, 92/93, 94, 96ML, 96MC, 96MR, 96MR, 96MC, 96ML, 96/97T, 98/99, 101, 105, 120/121, 122, 122/123, 124, 124/125, 125, 126, 126/127, 128, 128/129, 130, 130/131, 132, 132/133, 134, 134/135, 136, 136/137; Orientale Hotel 100; Photoshot 22; Villa Athena 103
Cover credits: (Main) Ruins of the Greek Theatre, *AWL Images*; (bottom) Harbour, Sicily, *Neil Buchan-Grant/Apa Publications* (back left to right) Etna, *Bigstock*; Ragusa Ibla, *Neil Buchan-Grant/Apa Publications*

Printed by CTPS – China
All Rights Reserved
© 2014 Apa Digital (CH) AG and
Apa Publications (UK) Ltd
First Edition 2014

DISTRIBUTION

UK, Ireland and Europe
Apa Publications (UK) Ltd
sales@insightguides.com
United States and Canada
Ingram Publisher Services
ips@ingramcontent.com
Australia and New Zealand
Woodslane
info@woodslane.com.au
Southeast Asia
Apa Publications (Singapore) Pte
singaporeoffice@insightguides.com
Hong Kong, Taiwan and China
Apa Publications (HK) Ltd
hongkongoffice@insightguides.com
Worldwide
Apa Publications (UK) Ltd
sales@insightguides.com

SPECIAL SALES, CONTENT LICENSING AND COPUBLISHING

Insight Guides can be purchased in bulk quantities at discounted prices. We can create special editions, personalised jackets and corporate imprints tailored to your needs.
sales@insightguides.com
www.insightguides.biz

INDEX

MAP LEGEND

- ● Start of tour
- → Tour & route direction
- ❶ Recommended sight
- ❷ Recommended restaurant/café

- ★ Place of interest
- ❶ Tourist information
- 🛉 Statue/monument
- ∴ Ancient site
- 🏛 Cable car
- 🏠 ⌂ Villa, refuge
- 🜊 Cave

- Park
- National park
- Important building
- Hotel
- Transport hub
- Shop / market
- Pedestrian area
- Urban area